ARMOR
in Korea

A Pictorial History

by Jim Mesko
illustrated by Don Greer

squadron/signal publications inc.

ISBN 0-89747-150-4

If you have any photographs of the aircraft, armor, soldiers or ships
of any nation, particularly wartime snapshots, why not share them
with us and help make Squadron/Signal's books all the more interesting and complete in the future. Any photograph sent to us will
be copied and the original returned. The donor will be fully credited
for any photos used. Please indicate if you wish us not to return the
photos. Please send them to: Squadron/Signal Publications, Inc.,
1115 Crowley Dr., Carrollton, TX 75011-5010.

Dedication

To Pat and Mom and Dad, for all they have done, and to those men and
women of the United Nations who fought for freedom in Korea.

PHOTO CREDITS

Bob Cressman	Simon Dunstan
Dana Bell	Ed Story
Paul Woolf	USMC
Mike Green	USAF
George Balin	USA
George Bradford	Canadian Public Archives
	University of Akron Library

Author's Note

On the morning of 25 June 1950 South Korea was brutally, and without
provocation, attacked by the North Korean Army, which had been armed
and trained by its mentor, the Soviet Union. For the next three years the
Korean peninsula was torn by fighting as savage as any that took place during
either world war. By the time an agreement ending the conflict was signed in
August of 1953, over three million soldiers and civilians had been killed or
wounded in the bitter fighting. Despite all this bloodshed, little was changed
aside from a slight difference in the boundary between North and South
Korea. Perhaps the only thing of lasting significance achieved by this conflict
was the awakening of the free world, especially the United States, to the very
real danger of communist aggression. It was also the first time in history that
free men throughout the world stood under one banner to defend a sovereign
nation against outside aggression without thought or consideration for
economic or territorial gains. This was perhaps the United Nations' finest
hour.

One aspect of the fighting in Korea which received little attention at the
time, and even less since, was the use of armor. To most people the Korean
War brings to mind infantry fighting infantry in hilly, mountainous terrain,
or of aerial duels between Russian MiGs and American Sabres. Yet armor
played a vital role throughout the war, especially during the early months of
the war, and often made the difference between victory and defeat. When
seen, it was usually the old M-4 Sherman tank of World War Two that was
usually seen in the official photos and film clips released. However, there was
a multitude of armored fighting vehicles (AFVs) which saw service
throughout the war. And many of these vehicles carried unique markings and
unusual camouflage schemes rather than the standard Olive Drab scheme
normally associated with armor of this war. With these considerations in
mind this book presents the vehicles of the Korean War with an emphasis on
the diversity of types and unusual color schemes.

INTRODUCTION

Since the late 1800s Korea has been a pawn in Russia's attempt to become a power in Asia. In the late 1890s Korea was under pressure from both Japan and Russia as they both sought to extend their influence in the area. This power struggle eventually resulted in the Russo-Japanese War in early 1904, when the Japanese bottled up and eventually destroyed the Russian Pacific fleet at Port Arthur. This coincided with a series of ground attacks launched from Korea against Russian forces in Manchuria. Following a string of bitter defeats on land, including the loss of Port Arthur, the Russians suffered a stunning naval defeat in the straits of Tsushima when the Baltic fleet was engaged by Admiral Toga and all but annihilated. This final blow forced the Czar to seek peace, and in September, 1905, through the efforts of President Teddy Roosevelt, a peace treaty was signed which effectively gave control of Korea to the Japanese.

For the next forty years the Japanese ruled Korea with an iron hand. Other than a few economic and civic improvements the Japanese did little to help the people of Korea. They took over all positions of authority and the Koreans became mere laborers in their own country. This treatment of the Korean people soon caused hatred to swell, and before long small guerrilla bands were operating against the Japanese. Most of these guerrillas were eventually driven out of Korea but found refuge in Soviet Siberia, where many of them were inducted into the Red Army, and many of these former guerrillas saw action in World War Two. These seasoned fighters eventually provided the nucleus of North Korean military leadership.

As the free world powers made plans in early 1945 at Yalta for the occupation of Japan and her empire, the question of Korea was raised by Stalin. After lengthy discussion with Roosevelt and Churchill it was agreed that Korea would initially be jointly occupied by Russian and US troops to disarm the Japanese and rescue any Allied prisoners held there. Elections would be held and Korea would take her place among the nations of the world as an independent country. After looking at a map of Korea it was decided that the Russians would occupy the northern part of the country, disarming Japanese troops north of the 38th parallel while US troops would disarm Japanese troops south of the 38th parallel.

In August of 1945, Russian forces moved into Manchuria and Korea against weak Japanese opposition. They took over half a million prisoners, most of whom were shipped to Siberia as slave labor. By the time US forces arrived in Korea in September, the Russians had effectively sealed off the 9 million Koreans north of the 38th parallel from their twenty-one million countrymen in the south. Rather than cooperating with American forces, the Russians did everything in their power to create trouble. Trade between the two zones was totally curtailed and electric power to the south was cut off, and lines of communication were disrupted. Instead of working to unify the partitioned country, the Russians set up a puppet government under the control of the Koreans who had served in the Soviet army and had received the "proper ideological indoctrination". With Kim Il Sung installed as their leader, these communist puppets soon liquidated (murdered) all opposition

to their rule. By the end of 1945 they held northern Korean in an iron grip, much to the delight of their Russian advisors.

In the south near chaos reigned as US troops muddled through their occupation duties. With few personnel trained in occupation duties, little was done to set up an effective Korean civil government. This was further complicated by the many political factions which existed in the south. Gradually order was restored in the south, and US authorities wished to hold elections and unify the country so the Koreans could work out their own internal affairs and facilitate the withdrawal of US troops. Unfortunately, the Russians had other ideas, and throughout 1946 and 1947 their intransigence made progress toward country-wide elections and unification impossible. Finally, frustrated by this Russian attitude, the United States took the problem to the United Nations. The UN resolved to hold national elections during the spring of 1948, but when the time came the Russians refused UN observer teams access to the north. Only in the south were free elections held. Syngman Rhee was elected president and the southern portion of the Korean peninsula was proclaimed The Republic of Korea, with Seoul as its capital. In retaliation for this, the communists proclaimed the Northern portion the People's Democratic Republic of Korea, with the city of Pyongyang as its capital. Kim Il-Sung was named its premier.

With Korea split into separate political entities, both the Russians and United States began withdrawing their occupation troops. The Russian forces were totally gone by the end of 1948, but the final American withdrawal was not completed until June 1949. Both countries left behind small advisory groups. The North Koreans, however, had received a great deal of equipment including armor and aircraft, as well as excellent training during the Russian occupation. In a short time this equipment and training would be put to use in an attempt to extend communist rule over the southern half of the peninsula.

Until the summer of 1950 Korea was a tiny country, unknown to the vast majority of the world. The sudden unprovoked attack by the communist North Koreans against the democratically elected government in the south brought this tiny, backward country into world prominence as the nations of the world took sides in the conflict. For the next three years Korea was a daily byline on the front page every major newspaper in the world and the subject of countless stories and debates on radio and television.

Even when the war ended during the summer of 1953, most people were still unaware of what Korea was like; as in most wars the battle made the news, not the battleground. Korea is a long peninsula, varying in length between 500 and 600 miles, with a width of 90 to 200 miles, except on its northern border where it widens out to nearly 400 miles along its boundary with Manchuria. Korean terrain is basically mountainous, with deep valleys and long, broad rivers. Many of these mountain ranges extend right to the coast on the eastern seaboard where there are few deep water ports. In the south and west these mountain ranges are not quite as severe and has resulted in a much more indented coastline with numerous deep water harbors. Though relatively small in land area, a total of approximately 85,000 square miles, it has a coastline nearly 5,500 miles in length.

In 1950 the total population of both North and South Korea was approximately 30,000,000 people. Of these, some 9,000,000 lived in the north while the rest inhabited the south. The north possessed nearly all the nation's natural resources of coal, iron, copper, graphite, and gold along with most of the country's hydroelectric power. Because of its proximity to the resources and hydroelectric power, most of the industry was located in the north. The south had few minerals and was the agricultural portion of the country.

An M-8 Armored Car from the 7th Infantry Division enters the town of Kyongsong with a Japanese liaison officer riding on the rear deck. These American troops were among the first to reach Korea following the Japanese surrender. (US Army)

(Above) Japanese troops march out of the town of Keijo to make room for the occupying American troops. (US Army)

These M-4 Shermans await inspection on the outskirts of Seoul in October of 1948. They belong to the 77th Tank Battalion of the 7th Infantry Division. When the unit redeployed to Japan these tanks were deactivated and replaced by M-24 Chaffee light tanks, which would not damage the roads or bridges in Japan. (US Army)

Because of abundant rainfall, especially during the summer monsoon, farmers were able to reap two harvests a year. Since they had little industry, the main products of the south were foodstuffs and textiles. Until the division of the country in 1945 the country ideally complemented each other and a brisk trade was carried on throughout the country. With the division trade dried up, nearly destroying the economy.

NORTH KOREAN ARMED FORCES

The North Korean armed forces left behind by the Russians were iron disciplined, well equipped, confident, and veteran-led, numbering some 135,000 men. It was divided into two groups, the Border Constabulary (BC) and the North Korean People's Army (NKPA). The Border Constabulary had been formed in September of 1945 from various anti-Japanese and communist guerrilla bands, and was initially used to help install the Soviet-indoctrinated leadership who arrived with the Russian occupation forces. At the time of its formation the BC numbered about 18,000 men, but by 1950, with the inclusion of regular police, and "thought" police, the total internal security forces under the control of the BC numbered some 50,000 men. Of these internal security forces only those men assigned specifically to the BC were organized as a combat force, and while acting in a security role they were actually crack combat troops. At the time of the invasion the BC consisted of five brigades, the 1st, 2nd, 3rd, 5th, and 7th, each of which varied in size and armament. The 1st, 3rd, and 7th were all trained and equipped as combat infantry units and were stationed just north of the border. The 1st numbered 5000 men, while the 3rd and 7th each had about 4000. The 7th was deployed in a line from the west coast to Haejer, where the 3rd's positions began, and ran from Haejer to the vicinity of Chorwon. The 1st was stationed on the east coast near the town of Kaesong. The 1st, 3rd and 7th brigades had six or seven battalions each, which contained three rifle companies each, and were supported by machine gun, mortar, and anti-tank units, along with the usual service units. Of the remaining two brigades the 2nd Brigade was the weakest with only 2600 men, who were divided into seven battalions, which guarded the the long northern border separating Korea from Man-

churia and Russia. The 2nd Brigade had little heavy equipment and very few mortars, machine guns, or anti-tank weapons. The last brigade, the 5th, had a strength of about 3000 men and was assigned to Pyongyang, the capital. Its primary duty was railroad security, and thus the unit had little need of heavy equipment or crew served weapons.

The North Korean People's Army (NKPA) was composed of eight infantry divisions at full strength, two infantry divisions at half strength, an armored brigade, and a number of separate infantry, armored, and reconnaissance regiments. Many of these troops had gained combat experience during World War Two and all had received intensive training under the Russians. During the early stages of the occupation this had been done by the Russian army. After the Russian withdrawal, over 3000 Red Army advisors remained behind to supervise the growing North Korean army. All units were trained in Soviet-style tactics and organized along standard Russian army lines. Each infantry division at full strength numbered 11,000 men organized into three regiments, each of which had three battalions. Included within the division were various support units, including an artillery regiment, a self-propelled gun battalion, and other service units such as medical, signal, anti-tank, and transportation. All equipment was Soviet supplied and mostly of World War Two origin.

The armored brigade was composed of three regiments equipped with T-34/85 medium tanks. Each regiment was further broken into three battalions, and each battalion was composed of three companies. The number of T-34s in the brigade totalled 120, while the independent regiment contained another thirty. Thus, the NKPA had 150 T-34s to spearhead their assault.

To provide air support for the ground forces, the North Koreans had a small air force of 180 aircraft: 40 fighters, 80 attack and reconnaissance planes, and 60 trainers. Their main job was to provide ground support since little aerial opposition was anticipated during the assault south.

The North Koreans also had a small navy equipped with sixteen patrol craft, a small force of junks, and a few coastal steamers fitted with light armament. The navy's main job was to land regular troops or guerrillas behind enemy lines, along with transporting supplies as the ground forces got further south. Again no significant opposition was expected.

By the middle of June, 1950, the North Koreans had made all the necessary preparations to invade South Korea. Large quantities of supplies and ammunition had been moved to dumps just behind the border. Artillery units were in position to fire on South Korean border positions and lines of communications. Approximately 90,000 men of the BC and NKPA along with all of the 150 T-34 tanks stood poised for the assault.

The order of battle was as follows:

In the forty-mile gap between Kaesong and Chorwon the North Koreans concentrated over half of their infantry and most of their armor. These forces were to converge on Seoul by attacking down the Uijongbu Corridor, the ancient invasion route which led right to the capital. Near Kaesong the 1st Division was poised for the drive on Seoul along the old highway connecting Pyongyang and Seoul. Assisting it would be the 6th Division positioned just north of the Ongjin Peninsula, with support from the 105th Armored Regiment. East of Kaesong, the main force of the North Korean attack was deployed for the invasion astride the Wonsan-Seoul highway. To the west of the highway lay the 4th Division while on the eastern side the 3rd was deployed. Each Division had an armored regiment to spearhead their assault, the 107th Armored being assigned to the 4th Infantry Division, while the 109th supported the 3rd. Further to the east of this main drive was the 2nd Division which had the city of Chunchon as its objective. It was anticipated that once Chunchon was taken the 2nd would then shift its attack toward Seoul and turn the city's defenses on the eastern flank. While the 2nd was taking Chunchon, the 7th Infantry Division was to capture the town of Hongchon, southeast of Chunchon. This attack was designed to cut any reinforcements from the south to Chunchon and trap any units retreating from the city. Rounding out the NKPA order of battle was the 5th Division stationed along the eastern coast. Supported by independent units and strong guerrilla forces, the 5th had as its goal the capture of Chumujin and Kangnung along the coastal highway. To achieve this, the 5th planned to carry out a series of frontal attacks and seaborne assaults to turn the flanks of the defenders. Because of the high Taebaek mountain range to the west of the coastal plain the North Korean drive in this area was isolated from the rest of the forces engaged in the attack.

The North Korean plan counted on three elements for success: surprise, speed, and the armored spearhead. Hopefully, the pre-invasion deployment would either go unnoticed or be taken as plans for another of the border raids, which the North Koreans had carried out rather frequently. If surprise could be achieved a speedy victory would forestall any outside aid from reaching the South Koreans in time to materially affect the outcome. The world would be presented with a fait accompli before anything could be done, and all Korea would be under communist control. The key element in this battle plan were the armored spearheads. The North had never used tanks in their border raids. The appearance of tanks was expected to shock and demoralize the South Korean defenders, who had no anti-tank weapons capable of stopping the T-34. The NKPA infantry was expected to mop up whatever resistance remained. The plan involved no complex maneuvers but relied instead on simplicity and overwhelming strength. It fit both the characteristics of the Korean terrain and the temperament of the North Korean forces. It came very close to succeeding.

SOUTH KOREAN ARMY

The army of the Republic of Korea had its modest beginnings in the year immediately after the initial occupation of Korea by US troops. Unlike their northern counterparts, the South Koreans did not have men to draw upon who had combat experience. The first unit formed was a constabulary force, authorized and established in January of 1946. However, this organization grew very slowly, and by January of 1947, only numbered some 5000 men. By April of the same year, however, it had doubled to 10,000, and this was increased to 15,000 in July. A little over a year later, in August of 1948, this force became the Republic of Korea (ROK) Army. From this point on the Korean Army grew rapidly. By March of 1949 it numbered over 60,000 men as the imminent withdrawal of American troops precipitated a drastic jump in strength. This did not include either the police or naval units, which raised the total number of men under arms to nearly 115,000. However, of this total force only about 50,000 were trained and equipped as infantrymen.

Upon the withdrawal of the last US troops, an advisory detachment of Army personnel began working with the ROK Army. Known as the Korean Military Advisory Group (KMAG), it operated under control of the American ambassador rather than the Army. Any decisions concerning equipment the Koreans were to receive had to be approved by the State Department. These decisions were usually based on political rather than military needs. The general feeling at the State Department was that the ROK Army should only receive defensive weapons, reasoning that if the ROK Army were equipped with tanks and aircraft the South Korean government might be tempted to reunify Korea by force. The politicians, of course, carried this policy to the extreme. The Koreans were not given tanks or aircraft, and in addition were denied weapons capable of stopping such equipment. They had no modern anti-tank guns, recoilless rifles, heavy mortars, medium

artillery, or anti-tank mines. The Korean infantry was mainly equipped with M-1 rifles or carbines, 60mm and 81mm mortars, 2.36 inch bazookas, 37mm or 57mm anti-tank guns, 75mm pack howitzers, and a few 105mm howitzers. However, some units fighting guerrillas in the south were equipped with a variety of weapons, including old Japanese rifles from World War Two. Requests from the Koreans and their advisers to alleviate this equipment deficiencies were turned down for either political or military reasons. This was done even though some American advisers warned that the Koreans would be unable to withstand a full scale attack with their current equipment.

Perhaps the most serious deficiencies which the Koreans faced was their lack of armor. In June the only armor the ROK Army had were twenty-seven M-8 armored cars and some M-3 half tracks. In October of 1949, the Minister of Defense had requested 189 M-26 Pershing tanks but this had been denied by the head of the US advisory team on the grounds that the Korean terrain did not lend itself to tank operations. It is interesting to speculate what might have happened in the early days of the war had the South Koreans had these tanks.

At the time of the invasion the ROK Army was organized into eight "combat" divisions, the 1st, 2nd, 3rd, 5th, 6th, 7th, 8th, and the Capital Division. At full strength each division was to have 10,000 men, but only the 1st, 6th, 7th, and Capital Divisions were anywhere near full strength. The other units were roughly 3000 men under strength. The eight divisions had a total complement of 98,000 men, of whom 65,000 were combat troops, with the remaining 33,000 being headquarters and service troops. Of these divisions only four, the 1st, 6th, 7th and 8th, were deployed along the front line facing the North Korean forces. They were deployed along the 38th Parallel from the west to the east. Holding a line from the coast to a point near the Uyongbu corridor was the 1st Division. The responsibility for guarding the corridor itself was assigned to the 7th Division. Further to the east, the 6th Division held the area around Chunchon. At the extreme eastern end of the line the 8th Division was positioned along the coast to cover both a frontal assault and any amphibious attacks behind the main line. The only other unit on the line was the 17th Regiment of the Capital Division which held the isolated Ongjin Peninsula far to the west of the 1st Division. Of the other four units only the Capital Division was near the front, being stationed near Seoul. The other three were scattered in the interior, either fighting guerrillas or conducting training. The 2nd was near Taejon, the 3rd at Taegu, and the 5th at Kwangjie. On 25 June the ROK Army was ill-disposed to meet a concentrated thrust by the North Koreans. ROK troop disposition was well known to the communists who had a reliable spy network in the south. Unfortunately this was not the case with the South Koreans who had virtually no intelligence-gathering agents north of the 38th Parallel. The end result was that on the invasion date the South Koreans were not prepared, except in one instance, to counter the savage attack launched by the NKPA.

Members of the South Korean Constabulary force receive training on a 57mm anti-tank gun at the US Weapons School at Taegu. This was the largest anti-tank weapon available to the Koreans at the time of the invasion. (US Army)

Korean troops inspect a 105mm howitzer, model M3. In many cases these were cast-off American artillery pieces, often with worn barrels, which were already inferior to the artillery supplied to North Korea by the Soviets. (US Army)

UNITED STATES FORCES

By the summer of 1950, the United States military forces were but a shadow of what they had been at the end of World War Two. The most powerful armed force the world had ever seen had, in the short span of five years, been reduced to a shell of its former self. This was most evident in the Army, which had dwindled to a little over 500,000 men. At the time of the North Korean invasion of South Korea, these half million men were divided among ten divisions, the European Constabulary, and nine regimental combat teams. With the exception of the European Constabulary, none of these units were up to their authorized strength. Most regiments had only two of the three battalions allotted them in their infantry, artillery, and armored units; further, most equipment was of World War Two vintage, and suffered from old age, especially communication equipment and ammunition. However, though the manpower shortage and equipment situation were bad, the Army's greatest weakness lay in its morale and discipline. When the atomic bomb ended the Second World War, self-styled strategists and politicians declared that the atomic bomb had made conventional warfare obsolete. With the rush to demobilize after Germany and Japan were defeated, the Army's strength was cut to the bone. To build it back after these massive cuts the Army downplayed its combat role and emphasized its career and training opportunities. This carried over into training, where recruits were given a much reduced regimen rather than the strict discipline required of an army in the field. By 1950 the US Army seemed to have forgotten that a soldier's job was to fight.

The Air Force, the prima donna of the new military strategist, had been able to withstand any serious erosion of its strength since it was now viewed as the main strike force whose primary goal was seen as waging nuclear war against the Soviet Union. By 1950 the Air Force was at a transition point between prop and jet-powered aircraft. Its main bomber strength was made up of the B-29 Superfortress from World War Two, the B-50 (an improved model of the B-29), and the new B-36 Peacemaker, a massive aircraft equipped with both prop and jet engines. Backing up this main force were the prop driven A-26 and the jet powered B-45 medium bombers. Though it still had large numbers of prop-driven F-47, F-51, and F-82 fighters in service with regular, reserve, and national guard units, the transition was to an all jet fighter force. Frontline units were equipped with the F-80 Shooting Star, developed at the end of the war. This, the first operational American jet fighter, was gradually being replaced by the F-84 Thunderjet fighter bomber and the F-86 Sabre fighter. However, these new fighters were only just coming into service; it would be several years before they would totally replace the older F-80s. Though the Air Force was assigned the task of supporting the Army in case of war, the force it possessed in 1950 was ill-suited for this role. Effective liaison between aircraft and ground units was nonexistent, and the hard-learned lessons of tactical air support of World War Two had been all but forgotten with the new emphasis on nuclear deterrence. While in somewhat better shape than the Army, the Air Force had some very serious defects which needed to be remedied before it was an effective force.

The Navy, too, had suffered a serious erosion of its strength following the end of the war. By 1950 the fleet was a skeleton of its wartime strength with most of the fleet carriers, battleships, and cruisers in mothballs. In the Far East there was one carrier, a few cruisers and destroyers, and some auxiliary vessels. The Navy, like the Air Force, was also in the midst of a change from prop aircraft to jet aircraft in its air arm. The F6F Hellcat and F4U Corsair fighters had been replaced by F2H Banshees and F9F Panthers, though the Corsair had received a reprieve as a fighter bomber. Backing up the Corsair

was a relatively new prop-driven fighter bomber, the Douglas AD Skyraider. Even though it had been cut back, the Navy still had a high level of morale and discipline. Its main goals were to keep the sea lanes open, interdict enemy lines of communication, and provide air cover and support for the fleet and Marine ground units. The Navy was somewhat better prepared to wage conventional warfare than either the Army or the Air Force.

The final component of American military strength, the Marine Corps, had also been cut drastically. From a peak strength of half a million men at the end of World War Two it had shrunk to 75,000 men by 1950. Only two divisions remained, both of which were understrength. And they too faced equipment problems. But whereas the Army had down-played its combat role, the Marines never forgot that their mission was to fight. This carried over into their training, and, more importantly, into their morale. The Marine Corps still emphasized "esprit de corps", that phenomenon which has always pulled the Marines through adversity when others fell apart. The Marine of 1950 was little different from those who fought at Beallou Wood or Guadalcanal, Wake Island, and Iwo Jima. He was proud of himself, his unit, and the Corps. This attitude gave him a tremendous advantage over his Army counterparts. Furthermore, Marines were backed by their own air arm equipped with Corsairs and Skyraiders. These airborne Leathernecks knew their job was to support Marines on the ground. The Marine Corps had pioneered close ground support, and with experience gained from World War Two and constant training, had developed the finest ground support air force in the world. Backed up by the Navy, the United States Marine Corps was a fighting force without equal.

At the time of the North Korean invasion the closest combat troops to Korea were four divisions on occupation duty in Japan, the 7th, 24th, and 25th Infantry Divisions, and the 1st Cavalry Division (Dismounted). Also close at hand was the 29th Infantry Regiment on Okinawa, and the 5th Regimental Combat Team in Hawaii. The only other ground unit in the Pacific area was the 1st Marine Division in California. The Army units in Japan were at approximately seventy percent of their combat strength. They had nowhere near their full complement of recoilless rifles, mortars, and machine guns. The units were also lacking in anti-tank mines and had none of the new 3.5 inch bazookas. Since it was feared heavier tanks would tear up the Japanese roads and cause the Japanese lightweight bridges to collapse, the divisional tank units were equipped with M-24 light tanks instead of the heavier M-4 or M-26 medium tanks.

The Army troops making up the occupation forces typified the general attitude of enlisted men in the Army at the time. They had little concern for their military duties and enjoyed the soft life and pleasures which were offered in Japan. Few, if any, thought they would ever have to fight. Even if a war did occur, they felt capable of handling anything since they were "Americans", and of course that meant "they were the best". Unfortunately there was no basis for this confidence. And while many of the officers and non-coms had combat experience, lack of discipline, which pervaded the lower ranks, prevented this asset from being fully exploited.

INVASION

During the rainy pre-dawn hours of Sunday, 25 June, 1950, the North Koreans began their attack with a massive artillery barrage. To the South Korean soldiers on duty the rumbling at first sounded like distant thunder, until high explosive shells began landing among their positions; only then did some of them realize that this barrage was more than a border raid. All along the front the alert was sounded but most of the troops had been given weekend passes. This seriously hampered any meaningful reaction to the invaders since many of the key personnel were on leave. Only the 6th Division, near Chunchon, was fully alerted and ready for battle.

In the far west, elements of the 6th NKPA Division and the 3rd Border Constabulary Brigade quickly overran the regiment holding the Ongjin Peninsula, then turned east to participate in the drive on Seoul. Northwest of Seoul, at Kaesong, the South Koreans suffered a major defeat during the opening hours of the campaign, when the North Koreans launched a two-division attack supported by tanks and aided by a regiment of infiltrators behind ROK defensive positions. This was the first instance that ROK troops came face to face with the Russian built T-34. Armed with obsolete 37mm anti-tank guns and 2.36 inch bazookas, the South Koreans were unable to stop these armored monsters. In desperation some soldiers threw satchel charges under the tanks, while others climbed atop them in an attempt to pry open turret hatches and throw grenades inside. Unfortunately such methods, though valiant, were no substitute for heavy anti-tank weapons. Those Koreans who tried such tactics were picked off by the accompanying infantry or machine gunned by other tanks. Within a short time the soldiers willing to try these suicidal attacks dwindled. Brushing aside this resistance the NKPA captured Kaesong and pushed the 1st Division back toward Seoul.

East of Kaesong the North Koreans mounted their main thrust down the historical invasion route to Seoul, the Uijongbu Corridor. The 3rd and 4th NKPA Divisions, each backed by a tank regiment of the 105th Armored Brigade, hit the ROK 7th Infantry Division with a devastating two-pronged attack. Under relentless pressure from the T-34s, self-propelled SU-76s, and waves of infantry, the ROK 7th Infantry fell back toward Uijongbu. Immediate reinforcements were requested by the division commander but by the end of the day the North Koreans were so close to the city that the inhabitants could hear the sounds of small arms fire.

While the 7th Division fought desperately to halt or at least slow down the communist drive on Seoul (one infantry company stood and fought on a hill above Seoul until the last man was killed), events to the northeast of the capital were upsetting the communists' carefully laid plans. In the Chunchon sector the commander of the 6th ROK Division had not allowed weekend passes for his troops. Instead he had ordered a full alert, and the unit, which had just gone through an intensive training program, was ready when the 2nd NKPA Division attacked. Fighting from prepared positions, the South Koreans threw back the initial communist attacks. Unsupported by tanks and fighting an alerted, entrenched foe, the North Koreans took heavy casualties and were unable to make any headway. After the division had been repulsed several times with heavy losses, the North Korean High Command realized this situation could impede the whole offensive. The 7th NKPA Division was shifted to the Chunchon sector. Arriving on the second day of the battle, the division was immediately thrown into the fierce struggle. The South Korean 6th stubbornly held on but by the end of the third day the flanks on either side of them gave way, and then collapsed. The 6th division was forced to fall back. However, this gallant defense held the North Koreans up for three days, and it, along with other such heroic actions of the ROK Army, would make a difference in the final outcome of the carefully prepared enemy plans.

As the NKPA drove deeper into South Korea the ROK High Command attempted to blunt the drive. The 7th Division counterattacked against the 4th NKPA with some initial success; unfortunately the 2nd ROK Division failed to hit the 3rd NKPA as ordered. This allowed the North Koreans to continue their drive on Seoul. By June 27th the North Koreans were so close to the capital that both the government and civil population panicked and fled the city. Long columns of soldiers, government officials, and refugees clogged the roads leading south. While much of the ROK army were engaging the North Koreans north of the city, the order was given to destroy the bridges over the Han River, south of the city. Before the troops could get across, the bridges were destroyed. This premature destruction of the bridges caused a military calamity for the South Koreans. All heavy equipment and artillery north of the river had to be abandoned, and many of the ROK soldiers were unable to find a way across the wide Han. By the end of June the South

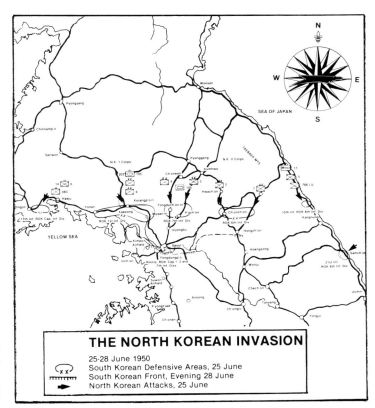

THE NORTH KOREAN INVASION
25-28 June 1950
South Korean Defensive Areas, 25 June
South Korean Front, Evening 28 June
North Korean Attacks, 25 June

Korean army numbered only 25,000 men, although eventually the number would double as stragglers worked their way south. The North Koreans could now overrun the rest of South Korea. The ROK Army was nearly incapable of effective defensive action; outside help was desperately needed.

Among the first US troops committed to Korea was the 507th Anti-aircraft Battalion. A small detachment from the unit, known as Detachment X, was airlifted into Suwon Airfield to provide protection for General MacArthur when he visited the front on 29 June. That afternoon the airfield was attacked and the unit destroyed or damaged two Yak fighters. In the background is a B-26 from the 3rd Bomb Group, an F-82 from the 68th Fighter (All Weather) Squadron, and the wreckage of a cargo plane. The weapon they are manning is an M55 mobile machine gun carriage with four .50 caliber machine guns. This was the same gun mount carried in the M-16 halftrack. (US Army)

(Below) An M-3 halftrack of the ROK Army waits in a small village while other vehicles pass. In the first days of the war the possibility of attack from the North Korean Air Force made it necessary to camouflage vehicles with foliage or straw to avoid detection. (US Army)

TASK FORCE SMITH

Upon receipt of word that South Korea had been invaded, the government of the United States immediately sponsored a resolution in the United Nations which provided military aid to the embattled nation. In a major diplomatic blunder the Russians were absent from the UN that day, and were unable to veto the resolution, which was passed by the General Assembly. President Truman then ordered American air and naval units to immediately aid the South Koreans, but held off committing ground forces in the hope that this commitment would be enough to do the job. Unfortunately, air power, despite all its potential, COULD NOT WIN A GROUND WAR BY ITSELF. By the end of June, with the fall of Seoul and the disaster at the Han River, Truman realized that the only way to avert defeat was to commit American ground troops, and he so ordered on 30 June. General MacArthur, commander of all US forces in Japan, ordered troops to prepare for movement to Korea. In an effort to prop up the shattered ROK army a small combat group was rushed to Korea as an "arrogant display of strength", in the words of MacArthur. This unit, from the 24th Infantry Division, was composed of two infantry companies under the command of Lieutenant Colonel Brad Smith, and received the designation Task Force Smith. After arrival in Korea on air force transport, the task force, reinforced by six 105mm howitzers, proceeded north toward Seoul. Numbering 540 men, they deployed north of Osan on 4 July, digging in on the ridges which ran along the side of the main road from Seoul to Oson. Since the Task Force had a total of only six anti-tank shells for the 105mm howitzers, all but one of the howitzers were placed in the rear to provide fire support. The remaining howitzer was positioned to cover the road in case tanks tried to force their way through the valley.

Early on the morning of 5 July an ominous rumble woke the sleeping Americans. In the distance, the men of Task Force Smith saw a column of thirty-three T-34 tanks from the 107th Tank Regiment advancing on their position. Artillery fire was called in but the high-explosive shells did little more than scratch the paint on the T-34s. As the tanks neared the Task Force's perimeter the GIs poured recoilless rifle and bazooka fire at them, but the tanks continued to advance. Finally, as the two lead T-34s pushed through the outer defenses they were stopped by anti-tank shells from the 105mm howitzer. Unfortunately, the howitzer soon used up the six anti-tank shells and had to switch to high-explosive rounds which proved to be totally useless. Within two hours the entire column of T-34's had pushed through Task Force Smith and were heading for Oson. Besides the two tanks destroyed by anti-tank shells, two more tanks were destroyed by high-explosive hits in the rear, and a few had received minor damage, but on the whole the 107th Regiment had come through the engagement in good shape. Task Force Smith lost surprisingly few men, even along the perimeter, but all their infantry vehicles were destroyed and two howitzers were knocked out. Within an hour of the armored attack Task Force Smith faced another enemy column, two regiments of infantry from the 4th NKPA Division. Fortunately, these regiments had only three tanks for support, and for a time the Task Force was able to hold its ground. But eventually the North Koreans were able to out-flank the American position. Confusion soon set in, and the unit attempted to retreat. Enemy fire quickly turned this retreat into a rout, with the panic-stricken troops abandoning their heavy weapons and even some of

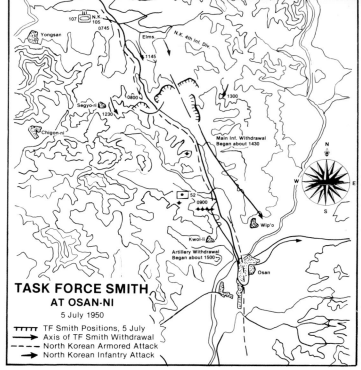

TASK FORCE SMITH
AT OSAN-NI
5 July 1950

ΤΤΤΤ TF Smith Positions, 5 July
⟶   Axis of TF Smith Withdrawal
----   North Korean Armored Attack
⟶   North Korean Infantry Attack

The first American tank to arrive in Korea was the M-24 Chaffee light tank. This M-24 advances toward the town of Chonui. The first engagement of the Korean War between U.S. and North Korean armor took place near Chonui on July 10th when M-24s engaged T-34s during a counterattack by an American infantry battalion. (US Army)

(Below) A camouflaged 105mm howitzer emplacement sits astride the road to the town of Chunan. Although a good artillery weapon, without special anti-tank shells these howitzers were ineffectual against tanks. (US Army)

their wounded. Eventually about two-thirds of the original force reached safety, but of the remaining men half were killed and the rest captured. The first contact between the North Koreans and American soldiers resulted in a decisive victory for the NKPA. It gave their morale a tremendous lift and caused American spirits to sink. Unfortunately, from the beginning Task Force Smith had little or no chance of success. Equipped with obsolete anti-tank weapons, no anti-tank mines, only a few 105mm anti-tank rounds, no armor, and no air support, the Task Force had been asked to do the impossible. Had any of this equipment been available the Task force would have fared far better. Poor discipline during the latter stages of the battle helped precipitate the rout which eventually occurred, and was a direct result of the training standards which the Army employed.

RETREAT

The defeat of Task Force Smith was the first in a string of victories which the North Koreans achieved over American troops during the long July of 1950. As US troops arrived in Korea they had arrogantly predicted that the enemy would retreat when they heard that there were American soldiers in front of them. After the defeat at Oson, it was American GIs that retreated when they found that an attack was imminent. In fact this time frame became known as the "bug-out" period because of the quickness with which American troops took to their heels. In all fairness, however, the tactical situations that American troops usually found themselves in were seldom conducive to military success. In an effort to blunt the NKPA drive, units were often committed piecemeal in company or battalion strength as soon as they arrived in Korea. They seldom had either artillery or tank support, and were usually unable to contact air support because of inadequate or nonexistent communications with the Air Force. In addition, none of their infantry weapons were capable of stopping the Russian-made T-34 except under the most favorable conditions. An urgent request was made to rush some of the new 3.5 inch bazookas to Korea; these heavier bazookas arrived in mid-July but saw little action before the Battle of Taijon.

In an attempt to shore up the crumbling defenses, the 78th tank Battalion was shipped from Japan. Equipped with the M-24 Chaffee light tank armed with a lightweight 75mm cannon, the battalion was thrown in the line near the town of Chonui on 10 July, where they supported elements of the 21st Regiment of the 24th Infantry Division. The Chaffees ran into T-34s of the North Korean 107th Tank Regiment and were able to destroy one T-34 for the loss of two M-24s. The next day, however, five more Chaffees were lost to artillery and infantry attacks. These losses quickly pointed up how vulnerable the M-24 was, especially to the heavily armed and armored T-34. From this point onward the Chaffee was used mostly in the infantry support role, and if enemy armor appeared, or artillery fire became probable, the M-24s were quickly pulled out of range. Such tactics did not encourage the infantry, who often followed the example set by the armor and also retreated out of range. Other US armored vehicles which were rushed pell-mell to Korea fared equally as badly as the M-24 Chaffee. The M-8 armored car was initially used by a number of reconnaissance units. Armed with a 37mm cannon, this vehicle and its utility version, the M-20, were of little value for front-line service and were quickly relegated to convoy duty, airfield security, and Military Police duties. The other armored vehicles which were initially

(Below) A large number of atrocities were committed against American and South Korean troops by the North Koreans. This prisoner was found murdered by the enemy after he and three other men had been captured. All four were found shot with their hands tied behind their backs. (US Army)

Camouflaged with pine branches, an M-24 sits in a defensive position while the commander listens for the sound of enemy planes. The hot Korean summer was hard on both the infantry and armor troops. This tanker has taken the opportunity to remove his shirt to take advantage of any slight breeze. (US Army)

used in any numbers were the M-15 A1, M-16, and M-19 self-propelled anti-aircraft mounts. The M-15 of early World War Two vintage was basically an M-3 halftrack equipped with a single 37mm cannon and two .50 caliber machine guns mounted in a revolving turret. The M-16, also based on the M-3 halftrack chassis, had a power-driven turret fitted with four .50 caliber machine guns. The M-19, based on the chassis of the M-24 Chaffee, was armed with two 40mm cannons in an open-topped turret. All these vehicles were initially deployed with the various anti-aircraft battalions which were rushed pell-mell from Japan. While none could stop the T-34, they proved very ef-

The crew of this M-24 have positioned their tank behind a low dirt bank for protection from enemy fire. The vehicle has been backed in so a quick retreat is possible, an all-too-common occurrence during the first months of the war. (US Army)

The crews of these M-8 armored cars zero in their cannons and machine guns at the firing range outside Taegu. They are part of a tank platoon which included the first medium tanks committed to the Korean fighting. By the end of July this unit was engaged in fierce fighting around the town of Chinju where 3 M-26 Pershings were lost due to faulty fan belts. (US Army)

fective in the infantry support role because of their high rate of fire. Because of its age, the M-15 was soon withdrawn, but the M-16 and M-19 would serve throughout the war.

In an effort to hold a viable defensive line against the advancing North Koreans, the commander of the 24th Infantry Division, General William Dean, positioned his troops along the Kum River north of Taejon. Across the river facing Dean's troops were the NKPA 3rd and 4th Infantry Divisions which Dean was trying to delay. Both North Korean Divisions had lost a good deal of their armored support to air attacks which had also succeeded in destroying much of their supplies. In addition, both enemy divisions had also suffered serious casualties in their drive south and were in need of rest and replacements. However, the need to keep the initiative pushed the divisions onward. The communists launched their attack on 14 July. For two days the battle raged, until the communists finally forced their way over the river and brought their T-34s into action. General Dean had not intended to hold Taejon if the North Koreans crossed the Kum River, but this changed when the commander of Eighth Army, General Walton Walker, asked him to hold

An M15A1 anti-aircraft halftrack moves up to support the 24th Infantry Division near the Kum River. This vehicle was armed with a 37mm cannon and two .50 caliber machine guns in a revolving turret. Though a good weapon against infantry and softskinned vehicles, it was not an effective anti-tank weapon. Because of this and its age the vehicle was replaced by more modern equipment such as the M19 40mm Gun Motor Carriage. (US Army)

The crew of "REBEL'S ROOST" pose in front of their M-24 after seeing action on July 10th. This is believed to be the first M-24 to see action against the North Koreans. The markings on the fenders indicate it is from the 24th Reconnaissance Company, 24th Infantry Division. (US Army)

This M32 recovery vehicle, based on the M-4 chassis, tows a disabled M-24 from the area south of Yenchon on 19 July. Both vehicles belong to the 79th Tank Battalion which was in support of the 25th Infantry Division. This unit was in action during the latter part of July in the defense of Sanju and Hamchang. (US Army)

(Left) The crew of this Chaffee positioned their vehicle under a tree to camouflage it from enemy observation and to get some relief from the sun. Though a good reconnaissance vehicle, the M-24 was totally outclassed by the T-34. It was not until the arrival of M-4, M-26, and M-46 medium tanks that American tankers were able to meet the T-34 on an equal basis. (US Army)

Mines were a problem to all vehicles. This truck has been severely damaged by a mine. In the background is an M-20 armored car and an M-39 armored utility vehicle, both of which saw extensive service early in the war. (US Army)

Taejon. Walker, a tank commander under Patton during World War Two, needed the time to bring in enough troops to establish and man a line of resistance along the Naktong River. Unless Dean could gain the needed time, the very real possibility existed that the North Koreans would push the American and ROK forces into the sea. Dean agreed, especially since he had some of the new 3.5 bazookas which he felt could stop the T-34. To encourage his men, and because of poor communications, Dean directed the rear-guard elements in Taejon himself. The enemy launched a two-pronged attack against the city on 19 July, and by the next day had broken through the American lines around the city. T-34s, without infantry support, roamed through the streets of the city, easy prey for infantry armed with the new 3.5 inch bazooka. Unfortunately, most of the GIs, still afraid of the big tank, could not be gotten out of their positions to attack the T-34s. General Dean himself eventually went "tank hunting", and after an hour of stalking a T-34 had the satisfaction of directing its destruction with the new bazooka. Eventually ten T-34s were destroyed inside the city, eight by bazooka fire, and air support killed at least another five outside the city. The North Koreans soon had Taejon effectively surrounded. Rather than lose what men he had left, Dean ordered a retreat, but this was hampered by numerous enemy road blocks. During the withdrawal Dean became separated from his main body of troops and was eventually captured by the North Koreans. Upon his release from POW camp three years later, General Dean learned that he had been awarded the Medal of Honor for his heroic actions in holding the North Koreans at Taejon.

South Korean troops manhandle a 57mm anti-tank gun into position on the northern outskirts of Andong. This important town was on the Naktong River, and during the last week in July was the scene of a fierce battle between the NKPA 12th Infantry Division and the ROK 8th Infantry Division. The town finally fell to the North Koreans on August 1st, but only after the South Koreans had inflicted serious losses on the attackers. (US Army)

(Left) This T-34 was one of seven destroyed by a combination of aircraft and infantry weapons by the 27th Infantry Regiment during the fighting around Poun. The T-34s were attached to the 2nd NKPA Infantry Division and are believed to be from the 203rd Armored Regiment of the 105th Armored Brigade.

The commander of this M-24 scans the horizon for signs of enemy activity. Because of their light armor, M-24s were usually positioned to take advantage of whatever protection the terrain would provide. (US Army)

The crew of this M15A1 dig their halftrack in for extra protection near the town of Kunchon. The vehicle belongs to the 92nd Anti-aircraft Battalion which was part of the 1st Cavalry Division. (US Army)

This M-20 armored car waits along a road while a stubborn ox is coaxed out of the way. The car is from the 8066th Reconnaissance Company of the 1st Cavalry Division, which in the last week of July was involved in the defense of the of Yongdong against the 3rd NKPA Division. After a two-day battle the town fell to the North Koreans when they were able to cut the roads in the rear of the 1st Cavalry's position. (US Army)

THE PUSAN PERIMETER

After the North Koreans broke the Kum River line, the last natural defensive position that could be held against the North Koreans was the Naktong River. General Dean's defense of Taejon had bought General Walker much of the desperately needed time; time that was used to bring in and deploy the 1st Cavalry Division and the 25th Infantry Division, which had been brought to minimum combat strength by cannibalizing the 7th Infantry Division. The new divisions were deployed and in action by 25 July, forming a defensive line north of the Naktong River, extending from west of the Taejon-Taegu highway to the Sea of Japan north of Pohang-dongo. As the bone-weary 24th Division retired to this line, the whole line began coming under pressure as communist units moved south. The fresh, but green, 25th Infantry Division was shifted south to meet an attack by the North Korean 6th Infantry trying to roll up the Eighth Army's southern flank. As the pressure increased it became obvious to Walker that the line would have to be shortened to the Naktong River.

In an effort to bolster defenses three M-26 Pershings, armed with 90mm guns, were rushed from Japan. Found in Tokyo at the beginning of the Communist invasion, in very poor mechanical condition, they had to be completely overhauled. By mid-July the work had been completed and the three tanks were rushed to Korea. Unfortunately, when the tanks were reconditioned, there were no fan belts for the engines and substandard ones had to be used. After a short period of running the tanks' engines, the fan belts stretched, causing the engine to overheat. New fan belts had been requested but before the new belts arrived, the 6th NKPA Division began an attack aimed at trying to turn the southern flank near the town of Chinju. On 28 July, the three Pershings were rushed by rail to the Chinju to support the 19th Infantry Regiment. While the Pershings sat in Chinju waiting for the fan belts to arrive, the town fell and American forces retreated again, leaving the three tanks isolated. Since the tanks could not make a forced march, the tank detachment commander, Lieutenant Sam Fowler, tried to get flatcars to evacuate the precious armor. The flatcars never showed up, so on the morning of 31 July, Fowler decided to try to save the tanks by moving them under their own power. Before the tanks could move out they became involved in a firefight with a North Korean infantry patrol and Fowler was wounded. After dispersing the enemy platoon, the tanks rumbled toward safety but were stopped by a destroyed bridge. While preparing to destroy the armor the tankers were again attacked by infantry and scattered. One tanker was able to start an M-26 and save a few of the crewmen, but fully half of the tankers were either killed or captured. The lone running tank eventually overheated and had to

be abandoned. Thus, the only medium tanks in Korea were lost.

However, on the same day the three Pershings were lost, the first M-4 Shermans arrived at the port of Pusan. These were from Company A of the 8072 Medium Tank Battalion recently activated in Japan. Within hours the Shermans were sent to the front, going into action the next day. Within a few days the remainder of the battalion arrived and its designation was changed by the Eighth Army to the 89th Tank Battalion.

On 1 August the 5th Regimental Combat team arrived and on the same day the 2nd Infantry Division began disembarking. The next day the 1st Marine Brigade came ashore. The Marine Brigade was understrength, but had 6500 first-class fighting troops, M-26 Pershing tanks, and Air Group 33 for air support. The North Korean attack on the southern flank was stopped cold by the Marines.

General Walker's tenacity had paid off. His forces had been able to hold the enemy long enough to set up a line along the Naktong, and though it could best be described as shaky, it held. On the northeast edge of the perimeter the reorganized ROK Army dug in, and although they were still lacking equipment the South Koreans were still very much in the fight.

The North Korean force which had crossed the 38th Parallel just a short month ago was worn, and the month-long drive had cost it huge casualties, including many of its combat veterans. But the North Koreans were still a disciplined, well-armed and determined foe, who still held the initiative. The North Korean leaders had counted on the campaign being short, but the resistance offered by the South Koreans and then the Americans had slowed down the timetable. Instead of a quick victory the campaign had become drawn out and allowed the US to rush desperately needed reinforcements and equipment to the peninsula. Besides surprise and speed, the enemy had counted on their massed T-34s to be the key to victory. The tank had indeed been instrumental in the initial victories of the North Korean Army, but large numbers of them had been lost to American fighter bombers, and its myth of

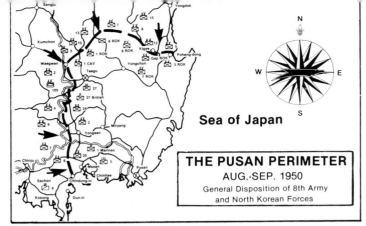

Often the North Koreans would infiltrate the thinly held lines around the Pusan Perimeter and set up roadblocks behind UN lines. Here, the crew of an M-20 armored car prepares to fire on a suspected enemy position overlooking a road to the front. (US Army)

invincibility was slowly being chipped away by the new 3.5 inch bazooka. The arrival of the M-4 Sherman armed with a high-velocity 76mm gun and the M-26 Pershing with a 90mm gun gave the Eighth Army weapons which could deal with the T-34. In addition the communists were at the end of a long supply line and their inability to supply their front-line troops was being felt. With the establishment of air superiority over the peninsula, the US Air Force, Navy and Marine fighter bombers had turned their attention to the numerous enemy columns pushing south. Large quantities of troops, supplies, and equipment, especially T-34s, had been destroyed by the roving aircraft. These losses had certainly cut into the strength of the NKPA divisions and reduced their efficiency; however, airpower had just as certainly not "beat the NKPA to its knees" as the Air Force claimed. The enemy held the initiative and fierce attacks were launched by the NKPA trying to drive the Americans into the sea. And they came within a hair of accomplishing their mission. It was only General Walker's tenacity and the doggedness of the American GI that prevented the disaster from happening. On 29 July Walker made the announcement that "There will be no more retreating...we are going to hold this line". And hold it they did.

Walker's Eighth Army was increasing in strength daily. The Eighth Army was able for the first time to present a front to the enemy, and while it was by no means continuous, being more a series of strong points from which troops could sally forth to put out one fire after another, it was a front even though there were gaps in it. Reinforcements were arriving every day, and more and more tanks were available to face the T-34. Better liaison with the Air Force and Navy (the Marines already had it) was being developed so that response time could be shortened to take advantage of the times when the enemy presented a good target. Finally, and perhaps most importantly, the soldiers themselves had begun to change. Instead of the ill-disciplined green troops who had been indiscriminately thrown into battle, the survivors of the fighting had acquired the experience which only combat can produce. Though these men may not have realized it they had changed. There were still instances when troops bugged out or even surrendered, but these instances were becoming rare. Evidence of what happened to prisoners at the hands of the North Koreans was becoming well-known throughout the ranks. American soldiers had been found murdered, their hands tied behind their backs, with a single bullet wound in the back of the head. In some cases they had first been subjected to brutal torture, including being bound and gagged with barbed wire, burned alive, and castrated. News of such atrocities did much to stiffen the backbone of even the most ill-disciplined soldier. All these factors helped improve the defenses of this small corner of southeast Korea, which was roughly 80 by 50 miles.

This M-4 Sherman was knocked out near the town of Masan. It appears to have been pushed off the road to make way for other vehicles. In their haste to abandon the vehicle the crew left the .50 caliber machine gun on its mount. (US Army)

The crew of this M-24 replenish their ammunition supply after the heavy fighting around Masan which lay to the west of Pusan. In August it was the scene of a desperate battle as the North Koreans attempted to take the town in order to clear the way for their drive to Pusan. Hard fighting by the 1st Marine Brigade (Provisional) resulted in the first victory over the North Koreans by American forces. (US Army)

The crew of this M15A1 pack up their gear prior to moving out to a new position inside the Pusan Perimeter. As the threat of enemy air activity diminished, anti-aircraft vehicles were used to support ground troops since their high rate of fire was excellent for giving the troops cover fire. Note the carbine hanging on the door and the helmet on the track. (US Army)

An M-19 anti-aircraft vehicle, armed with twin 40mm cannons, moves on North Korean forces near Yongsan. It is from the 82nd Anti-aircraft Battalion which had been shifted to the Yongsan sector in support of the 24th Infantry Division. (US Army)

VICTORY ON THE NAKTONG

One of the units which arrived to reinforce the Eighth Army was the 1st Marine Brigade, built around a nucleus of the 5th Marine Regiment. When it landed at Pusan on August 2nd it brought with it a company of M-26 Pershing medium tanks. The Marines had only received these a few days before they left the west coast of the United States, and had had no time to train with them. In fact the crews were only able to fire TWO rounds in practice before they embarked for Korea. They would not fire their weapons again until the tanks were at the front line. The brigade, when it disembarked, had a strength of roughly 6500 men, and was supported by its own air group. Most of the unit's officers and NCOs were combat veterans, and even some of the lower ranks had combat experience. Walker decided to use the Marine brigade as his trouble-shooter. He held them in reserve until the enemy threatened a break-through; the Marines would then be committed to throw the enemy back.

Immediately upon the Marine Brigade's arrival it was rushed to the southern flank to help stop a drive by the NKPA 6th Infantry Division on Masan. Though the Marines did not encounter any T-34s, their Pershings provided close support for the infantry and accounted for a number of machine guns and anti-tank guns. Soon after this threat had been contained the North Koreans launched a major attack along a bulge in the Naktong River, securing a bridgehead across the river. On 17 August the Marine Brigade counterattacked against enemy positions on Obong-ni Ridge, and the M-26s again destroyed at least a dozen anti-tank guns. As daylight waned the tanks withdrew to replenish their ammunition and fuel supply. At dusk, while the tankers were still replenishing their Pershings, a column of four T-34s from the 107th armored Regiment was spotted moving toward the Marine lines. Marine Corsairs destroyed the last tank in the column and dispersed the infantry who were riding on them. However, the remaining three T-34s continued on toward the Leathernecks' positions. While a call went back to the tankers, Marine infantry moved their bazookas and recoilless rifles to greet the enemy armor. When the tankers received word of the enemy tanks, they immediately wheeled about and moved out. The first Pershing arrived just as the T-34s began their attack. The lead enemy tank came around a bend in the road and was hit by bazooka and recoilless rifle

fire. Bursting into flames, it nevertheless continued forward and came face-to-face with the Pershing. The M-26 quickly fired two 90mm rounds into the T-34, which exploded in a ball of flames. The second tank, also hit by infantry weapons, came to a halt beside the burning one. Another M-26 had joined the first and the two of them fired thirteen rounds into the second tank before it too blew up. The last tank, blocked by the burning hulks of the first two, was hit by fire from every weapon possible and quickly erupted in flames. In five minutes the myth of the T-34's invincibility was shattered by Marine tankers and infantry. Hard fighting still remained ahead, but the Marines had given Walker his first clean-cut victory over the North Koreans.

After their first attack on the Naktong line the communists regrouped for another assault. On 1 September they launched an all-out attack against the perimeter. Again Walker called on the his Marine brigade to put out the fire. And again Marine Pershings encountered North Korean T-34s. In the fighting around the vital city of Myong-ni Marines destroyed four of the Russian-built tanks and captured a fifth. As fighting shifted back and forth the Marine tankers found themselves back at Obong-ni Ridge, the site of their first victory. Unfortunately, their earlier success was not to be repeated. The enemies again launched a tank attack against Marine positions but due to poor visibility and bad communications the Marine tankers were unaware of the attack. When the Pershings moved up to support the infantry their turrets were pointed away from the enemy tanks. The two lead Pershings were immediately hit by 85mm fire as they moved past the burnt-out hulks of the T-34s destroyed in the earlier battle. Both were knocked out, effectively blocking the road to the rest of the Pershings. However, Marine infantry began pouring bazooka fire at the two T-34s and a personnel carrier, eventually destroying them. These M-26s were the only ones lost by the Marines to enemy fire during the entire perimeter fighting. This battle was the First Marine Brigade's final action in the Perimeter fighting. Within days it was pulled out of Korea to rejoin its parent unit, the 1st Marine Division. Though the Pusan Perimeter was still in danger, one of the most brilliant plans in military history was about to be put into action and the 1st Marine Brigade was to be in the thick of it.

This M-39 utility vehicle and jeep were destroyed in the fierce fighting around Obong-ni. They are seen after American troops recaptured the area. The M-39 is from the 26th Anti-aircraft Battalion. (US Army)

On the night of 17 August the first encounter between T-34s and M-26 Pershings took place during the first battle of the Naktong Bulge. A column of four North Korean tanks tried to break through Marines holding Hill 125. Three of the four were destroyed by M-26, bazooka, and recoilless rifle fire, and another one fell to marine Corsairs. Here Marines inspect the remnants of the T-34s while awaiting the evacuation of their dead comrades. (USMC)

A Marine M-26 Pershing near the Naktong River during the large scale NKPA drive known as the Naktong Offensive. The jerry can on the turret has had the word WATER printed on it. The arrival of the M-26, along with the older M-4, spelled the end of the dominance that the T-34 had achieved over the UN forces. (USMC)

(Above) This T-34 was destroyed during the latter stages of the Naktong Bulge fighting. The top of the turret was completely blown off by the internal explosion, and the subsequent fire burned the rubber off the roadwheels. (USMC)

(Below) Korean troops from the ROK 8th Infantry Division fire 75mm pack howitzers against attacking elements of the 15th NKPA Division. The 8th was charged with the defense of Yongchon and although the town was lost, the South Koreans recaptured it and drove the North Koreans out with heavy losses. (US Army)

(Above) An unusual vehicle was this halftrack equipped with a 40mm cannon, which saw some service during the early days of the fighting. Known as an M15 "Special", it was basically an M15A1 with the cannon and machine guns being replaced by a single 40mm Bofors. This vehicle, minus its shield, sits in the town of Pohang-dong behind a makeshift camouflage of wall sections. (US Army)

(Below) A group of Marine M-26 Pershings provide cover for troops moving up to the front prior to an attack. Notice how a wire railing has been added to the fender for carrying extra machine gun boxes. Very early in the fighting it was found that as much extra ammunition as possible should be carried because of supply difficulties. (USMC)

These Marine M-26s and Army M-4s receive resupplies of ammunition during the fierce fighting which took place during the first week of September along the Naktong River. Extra gear is carried on the M-26, along with a wire ammo rack, and numerous holes in the fenders and storage boxes are from enemy machine gun fire. (USMC)

(Left) Two Marines advance past a burned out M-16 halftrack armed with quad .50 caliber machine guns. It appears that enemy fire set off the machine gun ammunition in the turret. (USMC)

From the heights overlooking the Naktong River the commander of a Marine M-26 fires the .50 caliber machine gun at enemy troops attempting to reach the safety of the far bank of the river. (USMC)

Mines were an ever present danger to tanks. This Marine M-26 lost its right tread to a mine while leading an advance against North Korean troops near Myong-ni. Extra gear is being carried over the entire tank. (USMC)

(Below) An M-19 from the 82nd Anti-aircraft Battalion sits on high ground above the Naktong River during the fighting around Yongsan in the first week of September. The crew has added sandbags to the gun shield to supplement the thin armor. The tubes atop the engine grill are extra barrels for the 40mm cannons. (US Army)

(Above)This M-4 dozer slid off the road after its left track was damaged by enemy artillery fire. It has the old type suspension rather then the more modern HVSS version. The tank was operating in support of the 24th Division, which was involved in a holding battle with elements of the 4th NKPA Division in the Yongsan-Miryang sector. (US Navy)

Marine Pershings move up in support of troops in the Obong-ni Ridge area during an attempt to dislodge North Korean troops. The enemy was able to hold on to this position but was so spent by the heavy fighting that they were unable to exploit their gains. This was the last time Marines participated in the fighting around the Pusan Perimeter; they were shortly withdrawn for the Inchon landing. (USMC)

INCHON AND THE PUSAN BREAKOUT

The Inchon landing was one of Douglas MacArthur's most brilliant pieces of military planning; this amphibious invasion completely turned the tables on the North Koreans and insured a United Nations victory in Korea. Originally conceived in July to get behind the advancing communist forces, MacArthur was unable to implement the plan when the Army units he had planned to use for the landings were diverted to help General Walker hold the enemy back at Pusan. As the situation stabilized around the perimeter, MacArthur was able to activate X Corps, made up of the 1st Marine Division and the 7th Infantry Division.

MacArthur decided to strike at Inchon because of its proximity to Seoul and its position astride the main enemy supply route south. Despite these tactical advantages Navy and Marine commanders were violently opposed to the site because of its physical features and difficulties. In the words of one commander, "If a list of the worst possible conditions for an amphibious invasion were drawn up, Inchon would have them all". But MacArthur felt that for these very reasons the enemy would not expect Inchon to be a target and would be taken by complete surprise. He finally won over the opposition with an eloquent argument for his case.

After a remarkably short pre-invasion build-up, the amphibious force was in a position off Inchon on September 15. The initial wave had the task of capturing Wolmi-Do Island, a rocky promenade which commanded the beaches along which the assault troops were to land. After a devastating bombardment Marines stormed the tiny island. Backed by Pershings and Sherman bulldozer and flamethrower tanks they quickly secured the island, and when tidal conditions improved, the remainder of the invasion force hit the mainland beaches on either side of the island. The Marines on Red Beach, north of Wolmi-Do, received support fire from Pershings on the island. However, the troops on Blue Beach, to the south, were unable to receive direct fire support from the tanks on Wolmi-Do. Instead they were supported by LVT(A)5s of the 56th Amphibious Tractor Battalion. Throughout the remainder of the day the Marines pushed forward against sporadic resistance. By the next morning the two invasion forces had linked up on the eastern outskirts of the Inchon, completely surrounding it. While Korean Marines mopped up resistance in Inchon itself, US Marines pushed on toward Seoul. As they advanced, a column of six T-34s was spotted by Marine Corsairs near the village of Kangsong-Ni and attacked. Two or three tanks were destroyed in the initial air strike but in the second air strike the same knocked-out tanks were hit again, causing the pilots to erroneously assume they had destroyed the entire column. When two Marine Pershings crawled atop a knoll overlooking the area, their crews were surprised to see three T-34s waiting in ambush for the approaching Marine column. The two Pershings immediately opened fire, destroying all three of the enemy tanks before their crews could even traverse the turrets.

The next day was more of the same. Early on the morning of 17 September a column of North Korean T-34s was spotted moving toward Marine positions which were now south of Ascom City. These tanks were from the NKPA 42nd Tank Regiment, the same unit which had lost six T-34s the day before. As the Marines watched, the enemy column advanced down the road totally unaware that they were moving within range of every anti-tank weapon the Marines possessed. The infantry riding atop the vehicles were eating their breakfast, which for most would be their last meal. The Leathernecks held their fire until the column had passed by their forward positions. When the T-34s were sandwiched between the Marine positions the order was given to open fire. All hell broke loose. Bazookas, recoilless rifles, 90mm cannons, and small-arms fire smothered the enemy column. Within minutes all six tanks were destroyed and over 200 of the accompanying infantry lay dead. Marine casualties—one wounded! This victory was one of the most stunning achieved during the entire war, and was considered an almost perfect textbook example of cooperation between armor and infantry anti-tank weapons.

While the Marines advanced toward Seoul, the other half of X Corps, the 7th Infantry Division, came ashore and moved to cover the Marine's right flank from attacks from the south. Supported by the 73rd Tank Battalion, the 7th Division moved toward the Seoul-Suwon highway. After having a number of tanks damaged by mines, the highway was reached and an advance unit was sent south to secure Suwon airfield. Without maps, the unit passed the airfield in the dark and pushed on south, passing out of radio range. Task Force Hannum was dispatched to find the unit in the dark, but when it reached Suwon it lost a tank to a T-34 lying in ambush. Rather than risk another ambush the force dug in for the night. Further south the other unit became engaged in a night battle with a column of T-34s which entered their perimeter by mistake. Two of the enemy tanks were destroyed at point-blank range before the other two managed to make a fast retreat. At dawn both American forces met and were able to secure Suwon airfield without

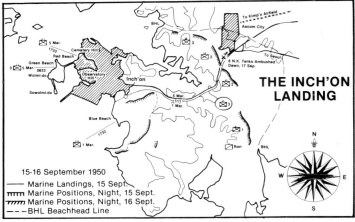

THE INCH'ON LANDING

15-16 September 1950

— Marine Landings, 15 Sept.
ᴍᴍ Marine Positions, Night, 15 Sept.
ᴍᴍ Marine Positions, Night, 16 Sept.
--- BHL Beachhead Line

further enemy resistance.

As X Corps expanded its bridgehead and the Marines pushed toward Seoul, the second part of MacArthur's plan was being undertaken. In an attempt to catch the North Korean Army in a vise he had ordered the Eighth Army to break out of the Pusan Perimeter and link up with X Corps. The breakout was planned to follow by one day the Inchon landing in the belief that the landing would raise the morale of the Eighth Army and at the same time crack the morale of the communist troops. Unfortunately North Korean troops did not learn of the invasion until three or four days after the landings. During the first few days of the break-out attempt the North Koreans were still attacking along most of the perimeter, preventing General Walker from sufficiently concentrating his forces for the breakout.

On the morning of 16 June, American and ROK divisions began their attack, supported by tanks, artillery, and aircraft. In some places the units had to beat off NKPA assaults before they could launch their own attacks; at the end of the first day few significant gains had been made. On the 21st Walker still could not punch a hole in the North Korean ring around his forces. During the next few days, as the North Koreans began to withdraw, their lines began to rupture. Walker was able to push tank-led motorized forces through the breaks to exploit the North Korean confusion. Once initial local resistance had been overcome, these task forces fanned out in the enemy's rear, raising havoc. Hammered by tanks, artillery, and fighter bombers the North Koreans retreated in disarray. Two regiments of the NKPA 105th Ar-

Marines aboard an invasion ship prepare tank ammunition for their Pershings. The round tubes in the foreground are the casings which the 90mm ammunition came in. Each tank carries a large amount of extra machine gun ammunition on the fenders. (USMC)

(Above) Amtracs of the 5th Marine Regiment move through a town on the banks of the Han after a successful crossing against enemy forces. This version of the amtrac, an LVT-3, does not have rear hatches. Versions which did were designated LVT-3C. Both saw service in Korea. (USMC)

A Marine dozer tank crawls up the banks of the Han River after being transported across the river on a pontoon barge. Armed with a 105mm howitzer this type of tank was used for close infantry support where its howitzer and dozer blade were invaluable in rooting out North Korean soldiers from bunkers and pillboxes. (USMC)

positions along the northern outskirts of the city. By 25 September Seoul was completely surrounded, except for a small portion in the northeast; there were not enough troops to cover this gap.

The main assault against the capital began on 25 September when the 1st Marines launched a drive toward the heart of the capital. Enemy resistance, however, was fierce throughout the day as the North Koreans bitterly fought the Marines for every yard of ground. By the end of the day the advance had only progressed a short distance into the city. Late that night the 25th NKPA Brigade launched an attack supported by T-34s and SU-76s against Marine lines. Fortunately part of this force ran afoul of a Leatherneck roadblock, where one of the tanks was destroyed. This alerted the main body of the Marine force and when the North Koreans attacked, the Marines blasted the enemy with mortar, artillery, bazooka, and recoilless-rifle fire. When the sun came up, the wreckage of seven tanks and two self-propelled guns were counted in and around Marine positions.

While the enemy was still reeling from these losses the Marines launched the final assault to capture Seoul. Elements of the 32nd Regiment held onto positions overlooking the eastern part of the city while the 1st and 5th

Marines pushed toward the center of the capital. The North Koreans resisted fiercely from behind numerous barricades of dirt-filled rice bags. These barricades, eight feet high and five feet wide, were set up at most intersections and were defended by infantry, machine guns, anti-tank weapons and mines. Each barricade was a battle in itself. Tanks were instrumental in breaching these obstacles. After engineers had removed any mines, the M-26s rolled forward to suppress machine-gun fire, while infantry closely supported the tank to prevent enemy soldiers from getting close enough to use hand-held weapons. One North Korean did manage to get close enough to throw a satchel charge onto the engine compartment of a flamethrower tank and even escaped to tell about it. The charge totally wrecked the tank, but the crew escaped without serious injury. This was the only tank which was lost to infantry action during the battle. Fighting of this nature continued for the next two days, until 28 September, when Seoul was declared secure, even though small bands of enemy soldiers still lurked in the ruins, and forces outside the city continued to make attacks against the Marine perimeter. The next day General MacArthur and Syngman Rhee officially took possession of the city and raised the Korean and American flags over the Government Palace.

While elements of the 5th Marine Regiment crossed the Han north of Seoul, the 1st Marine Regiment pushed toward the town of Yongdung-po, which sat across the river from the capital. Marine flamethrower tank has the weapon mounted coaxially with the 105mm howitzer in the turret. This version of the M-4 received the designation POA-CWS-H5. (USMC)

(Left) Amtracs from the 1st Amphibious Tractor Battalion move inland after crossing the Han River west of Seoul. This unit had helped carry members of the 5th Marine Regiment across the river on 20 June for the final drive to retake the South Korean capital. (US Army)

Within Seoul the North Koreans hung on bitterly and close-in fighting was the order of the day. A Marine Pershing from the 1st Tank Battalion, Company B, advances down a bullet-riddled street during the recapture. In the background can be seen pictures of two North Korean heroes, Stalin and Kim Il Sung, both of which were responsible for millions of people being butchered. (USMC)

To bring heavy equipment over the Han, a pontoon bridge was laid down as soon as the northern bank of the river was secure. SEX BOX, an LVT-3, has just been used by its crew to carry a cable over the river to help secure the bridge. (US Army)

(Right) An M-4 supports elements of the 32nd Infantry Regiment during the fight for Seoul. Tank is believed to be from the 77th Tank Battalion. Note how the infantry keep a wary eye to the sides and rear for any North Koreans who have laid low to backshoot at them. (US Army)

In the bitter street fighting the North Koreans employed their few armor reserves to no avail. Vast numbers of North Koreans were either killed or captured along with large amounts of weapons and ammunition. This SU-76 and T-34 were among the equipment captured by the Marines. (USMC)

ACROSS THE 38TH PARALLEL TO PYONGYANG

As X Corps in the Seoul-Inchon area linked up with the Eighth Army's tank-led task forces from the south, the North Korean Army began to disintegrate. Throughout the summer the NKPA had received few replacements and only small amounts of equipment and ammunition, due largely to their long supply lines and the incessant aerial attacks of UN aircraft. With their supply lines totally severed by the Inchon invasion, the communists were in dire straits. Wholesale panic set in as the North Koreans tried to pull back before all avenues of escape were blocked. Harried constantly by fighter bombers and the advancing Eighth Army, the NKPA fell apart. Entire units simply melted into the countryside; some tried to get back across the 38th Parallel while others began carrying out guerrilla warfare, and thousands surrendered.

The NKPA had little armor left. Most of their T-34s had been destroyed, although a few SU-76s still remained. These were used in fixed defensive positions to temporarily halt advancing American armored forces. The usual tactic was to site the vehicle in a position which covered a likely avenue of approach by US armor. From these positions the well camouflaged SU-76s hoped to ambush the first vehicles of an armored force and possibly destroy one or two of the lead tanks before they were spotted. Once their position was spotted, however, the enemy knew the Americans would smother the area with firepower. The North Korean crews would quickly abandon a position after disabling a vehicle or two, before they themselves came under fire. US tank crews learned to counter this tactic by firing on any likely ambush position in the hopes of blowing away any camouflage cover or causing the North Koreans to fire prematurely and give away their position. Even though the 76mm gun of the SU-76 could knock out an M-4 the vehicle's thin armor was of little value against large caliber weapons; once the enemy lost the element of surprise he had little hope of doing lethal damage before being destroyed by return fire.

As the North Koreans fell back northward, plans were made for the final destruction of the North Korean Army and the unification of all Korea under President Syngman Rhee. Receiving Truman's approval to cross the 38th Parallel, MacArthur formulated his strategy for victory. Rather than combine X Corps and Eighth Army under one joint command he decided to maintain each formation as a separate field command. Despite objections to this, MacArthur felt that supply and geographical conditions made this arrangement necessary. He decided to pull X Corps out of Inchon and use it for an amphibious assault on the Port city of Wonson on the east coast. The Eighth Army would continue to advance north of Seoul toward the North Korean capital of Pyongyang. Because of the high mountain range which ran along a north south axis through northern Korea, it would be impossible to maintain a continuous front during the push toward the Yalu River. MacArthur felt that two separate commands, one moving along the east coast, the other advancing up the western side of the peninsula, was the best option under the circumstances. Carrying out his plan meant the removal of X Corps from the battlefield for two weeks while the force moved by sea to Wonson. This caused many complaints from his field commanders, but in the end MacArthur's decision stood.

As X Corps prepared to re-embark, elements of the Eighth Army moved past Seoul towards the 38th parallel. On the east coast ROK army units pushed northward in trucks or on foot in pursuit of the retreating communists. By the end of the first week in October, elements of the 1st Cavalry Division had crossed the old border and were also heading toward the enemy capital.

Enemy resistance near the town of Kumchon was especially fierce. In a desperate effort to stop the cavalrymen, the North Koreans committed some of their remaining T-34s and Su-76s. In a series of pitched battles the three regiments of the 1st Cav tried to close a giant pocket around the enemy forces. The communists violently resisted this envelopment and a large number of enemy troops managed to escape the trap. In one action a column of T-34s tried to dislodge the 8th Cavalry Regiment. One enemy tank, despite being hit three times, kept ramming an American tank until a fourth shot finally destroyed it. During this particular battle the enemy lost eight T-34s without inflicting losses on the 70th Tank Battalion. After a week of heavy fighting Kumchon fell on 4 October. After the fall of Kumchon the Eighth Army began moving up men and material for the capture of Pyongyang, the North Korean capital.

While the 1st Cav was locked in the fierce struggle for Kumchon, X Corp embarked from Pusan and Inchon for the east coast landings. Due to extensive mine fields in Wonson harbor the landing was delayed while the mines were swept. While the minesweepers were working, Wonsom was captured by advancing ROK units, alleviating the need for an amphibious assault. The 1st Marine Division finally came ashore on 26 October, and the 7th Infantry Division was shifted north to land at the town of Iwon. By the second week of November the division was completely ashore except for its tanks. Initially, MacArthur had planned for X Corp to push westward to help secure the 8th Army's right flank. However, crumbling enemy resistance, geographic considerations, and supply problems caused him to change his plans. In conjunction with the ROK divisions X Corps was ordered to advance toward the Yalu River rather than support the Eighth Army.

While this redeployment was taking place, the Eighth Army began preparations for the final push on Pyongyang. As enemy resistance stiffened north of Kumchon, General Walker brought up the 24th Infantry Division on the left flank of the 1st Cavalry, and also moved the 27th British Commonwealth Brigade up in support of the Cavalry Division. In addition elements of the 1st and 7th ROK Divisions were moved up on the 1st Cav's right flank. Confused fighting erupted around the town of Sariwon as American and British troops moved into position. After a wild night of hand-to-hand fighting, large numbers of North Koreans began surrendering to US forces. As a result of this it became apparent that the enemy had little strength left to effectively defend Pyongyang. Given the forces advancing on them the North Koreans were more intent on moving what few troops they had left north, than in holding onto their capital.

A race soon developed between the various divisions to see who would be the first in Pyongyang. With the support of M-46s from C Company of the 6th Tank Battalion, the 1st ROK Division appeared to have the best chance for this honor. However, at the town of Kojodong, six miles outside the capital, the communists committed some of their remaining SU-76s in an attempt to halt the South Koreans. Though the position was eventually overrun, this resistance delayed the ROKs enough that the 1st Cavalry Division was able to catch up with them. Both units moved almost simultaneously into the city late on the morning of 19 October. In fact, the race was so close that neither unit was officially given credit for being the first in Pyongyang. Throughout the remainder of the day American and ROK troops continued to flush out small bands of the enemy and by the end of the day the city was firmly in UN hands. During the next few days UN forces spread out around the surrounding countryside to mop up any stragglers and secure the capital's seaport of Chinnampo. This was accomplished with little fighting; what remained of the NKPA had fled north to regroup along the Manchurian border.

The landing at Wonson was unopposed; yet, as in any such endeavor, something always goes wrong. The crew of this LVT help pull a jeep ashore which inadvertently got unloaded in water a little too deep for it. The biggest problem faced at Wonson was a vast array of mines. (US Army)

(Right) Following the link up of the Army and Marines, the 1st Marine Division was withdrawn and shipped by sea to the east coast of Korea, where they landed at the port of Wonsan. Much to the Marines' chagrin, ROK troops had already captured the port and the Leathernecks were forced to wait in the harbor until the port was swept clear of mines. This Marine amtrac moves inland after the Marines were cleared to hit the beach. Note the profusion of markings for tactical recognition. (USMC)

(Below Middle) An M-4A3 from the 5th Regimental Combat Team passes a knocked out T-34 near Kumchon. Note how much higher the Sherman is than the T-34. (US Army)

(Bottom) Following the landing at Wonsan the Marines moved overland to the port of Hungnam and set up a base of operations. These Marines use a Weasel to lay telephone wire on the outskirts of Hungnam. (USMC)

As the Marines moved north from Hungnam they captured the town of Hamhung, an important railroad center along the coastal plain. This Leatherneck stands guard over four SU-76s left behind by the retreating North Koreans. Some of these captured weapons were turned over to the South Koreans and used against their former owners. (USMC)

THE CHINESE INTERVENE

Throughout the long summer of 1950, the communist leaders in Russia and China sat back and waited in anticipation of the eventual subjugation of another country for communism. However, the reversal of the fortunes of their surrogate during the autumn caused the leadership in the Kremlin and Peking to begin calling for the United Nations to stop its aggression against the "innocent and peace loving people of North Korea". While the Russians confined themselves to mostly bombastic rhetoric, as UN forces moved deeper into North Korea the Chinese became more explicit. They flatly stated that unless UN forces stopped "...their aggression at the 38th Parallel, Chinese volunteers would be allowed to aid their comrades against the United States and its vicious allies." The UN chose to ignore this warning as little more than propaganda. MacArthur felt the Red Chinese would commit only token forces as a face-saving gesture rather than carry out a full-scale intervention. The UN and MacArthur were both wrong.

In preparation for the final push of the war, UN forces had been split into two forces separated by a mountain range. On the east coast, X Corps was given the job of pushing to the Yalu to cut off the enemy supply lines along the Manpojin-Kang-gye-Hurchon axis. On the west coast the Eighth Army was to strike for the Manchurian border, destroying the remainder of the North Korean army. The terrain through which these forces had to advance was mountainous with few roads, with their movements often being restricted to long columns of men and vehicles along a single muddy road snaking through deep mountain valleys. There was a fifty-mile gap between the X Corps and the Eighth Army, which was covered only by occasional aerial reconnaissance. Despite the dangers such conditions presented, MacArthur decided to push ahead and try to finish the war by Christmas. The General was confident that the North Koreans could not react in any appreciable strength and that the Red Chinese would not react in strength; he felt the advantages of this final assault outweighed the danger of the conditions.

Unknown to UN intelligence Red Chinese troops had already begun entering North Korea before the fall of Pyongyang. More and more Chinese troops slipped into northern Korea as the Eighth Army continued to advance North and X Corps landed its troops at Wonson. The 1st Marine Division drove toward the Chosin Reservoir area and the 7th Infantry Division pushed toward the Yalu River in support of the ROK Capital and 3rd Infantry divisions. Scattered intelligence reports of Chinese troops in northern Korea were dismissed as minor face-saving reinforcements for decimated North Korean units.

The Eighth Army still ran into occasional pockets of stubborn resistance. On 29 October near the town of Chongju elements of the 89th Tank Battalion, and the Commonwealth Brigade ran into a strong enemy position defended by T-34s and SU-76s. During the fight four tanks and self-propelled

guns were destroyed. After dark communist infantry supported by armor hit the American and Australian lines. Bazooka fire destroyed three T-34s while Allied tanks helped repel the ground assault. Two nights later the North Koreans again tried to destroy the task force with T-34s, SU-76s and an infantry battalion. During the early stages of the fighting the American tanks were hit by a number of rounds which did little damage. Returning the enemy fire, the M-4s were able to destroy five T-34s and an SU-76 by firing at their muzzle flashes. The next day two more tanks were destroyed by aircraft, while another two were captured on flatcars at a small rail yard. On 1 November near Chonggo-dong, a battalion of the 24th Infantry Division and C Company of the 6th Tank Battalion were hit by a North Korean battalion supported by T-34s. In a half-hour fight all the communist tanks were destroyed. This would be the northernmost penetration of the Eighth Army.

Ominous events began taking place on the Eighth Army's right flank where the ROK II Corps had pushed to the Yalu River. On 26 October the Red Chinese launched a massive attack on the ROK 7th Regiment, which nearly annihilated the South Koreans. The 7th had apparently gotten too close to a major Chinese staging area; wishing to keep their movements a secret, the Red Chinese nearly wiped out the regiment. Three days later two more ROK regiments broke under huge Chinese attacks and by 1 November the entire ROK II Corps had been driven back, exposing the right flank of the Eighth Army. More attacks followed as the Chinese hit individual units strung out along narrow roads between the steep mountains.

The Chinese had not committed enough troops to "save face"; over 500,000 Chinese troops had silently slipped over the border to battle the advancing UN forces. Unencumbered by tanks or heavy artillery, these units had moved only at night. Soldiers carried only cooked food so fires did not have to be started and great pains were taken to erase all traces of their passing before daybreak brought possible detection by roving aircraft. The Chinese forces were able to move into positions surrounding the UN forces without being spotted, and achieved one of the greatest tactical surprises in modern warfare. After carrying out attacks on the ROK regiments, elements of two Chinese Divisions then carried out their first large-scale attack on the Eighth Army. On 1 November at the town of Unsan, they hit the 8th Cavalry Regiment from three sides. Fierce, hand-to-hand fighting took place until the Americans, low on ammunition, were forced to retreat. Only when the regiment moved south and ran into Chinese roadblocks did the regiment realize that it was "surrounded and knee-deep in Chinese". Attempts by the 5th Cavalry to break through were to no avail; the 8th Cav was forced to break into groups of twos and threes to get through the Chinese lines. During the fighting nine tanks were either destroyed or abandoned, along with large quantities of other equipment. Though the tanks did prove extremely valuable during the battle, confinement to the narrow roads limited their usefulness, while exposing the tanks to enemy fire. This small action was but a taste of what was to come as the Chinese literally began enclosing UN forces inside a sea of Chinese troops.

With the entry of the Chinese into the war the entire tactical situation changed overnight. Faced with a new fresh foe, UN forces had to fight for their very existence. This M-19 from the 7th Infantry Division fires on Chinese positions near the town of Kapsan, only 30 miles south of the Yalu. It's obvious from the extra gear on "OUR LADY", the crew did not believe in traveling light. (US Army)

The crew of this M-19 watch attentively for any sign of enemy movement in the hills overlooking their position. The .50 caliber machinegun mount on the front plate was seldom used since there was no protection for the gunner while firing the weapon. Note the raised windscreen and wiper for the driver. (US Army)

RETREAT

During the last week in October and the first week in November fighting raged between elements of the Chinese Army and Walker's Eighth Army. Though X Corps experienced some fighting, particularly the Marines in the mountains south of Chosin Reservoir, these actions were nothing like the vicious fighting which occurred along the Eighth Army's front. Then suddenly the Chinese melted away, leaving no trace of where they had disappeared. Though the field commanders were leery of a possible trap, MacArthur ordered the drive to continue so the war could be finished before Christmas.

In the east ROK units advanced toward the border with Russia, while a regiment of the 7th Infantry advanced all the way to the Yalu, reaching the river on 21 November. On their left the Marines cautiously moved along a narrow single-track mountain road toward the Chosin reservoir. The Marine commander, General Oliver Smith, ordered his regiments to move cautiously and take whatever precautions they felt necessary. Smith knew from various reports and prisoners that Chinese forces lay in wait, and he refused to recklessly speed up his advance. On the Eighth Army's front, General Walker had to spread his units out as the terrain began to widen in this area of the peninsula. His main worry was the ROK II Corps which covered his right flank. These troops had already been hit hard and he was deeply concerned over their possible performance, especially since nearly sixty miles of mountains separated his army from X Corps.

Hampering both the Eighth Army and X Corps was the beginning of the Korean winter. Rarely had American troops faced such bitter conditions.

Rising off the Manchurian plain, a bitter, howling wind swept down on the desolate mountains of northern Korea, bringing raw cold and snow. Temperatures dropped ten to thirty degrees below zero. Under such conditions weapons failed to function and vehicles broke down. Tanks had to have their engines started every few hours to charge the batteries. The cold made such simple things as refueling or replenishing ammunition a tedious task since a tanker dared not remove his bulky gloves; if he did, frostbite was only a minute or two away. Nor could he lay an unprotected hand on the surface of his tank; if he did and tried to pull it away, he would leave bloodied flesh on the armor. Movement on the icy roads became a nightmare. The metal tank treads were unable to grip the hard, frozen surface; tanks often slid helplessly off the icy roads. Steep roads were totally impassable to vehicles unless improvised methods were used. Some units poured anti-freeze on them, while others covered the surfaces with fuel and lit it.

Under these conditions MacArthur ordered the final push to get underway on 24 November. Behind a massive artillery barrage the Eighth Army moved out. At first the tank-led columns moved quickly, encountering only light resistance. For two days the army advanced, gaining ground easily. Then on the night of 26 November all hell broke loose; 250,000 Chinese troops rose out of their hiding places to spring one of the largest ambushes in modern military history. The Chinese hit the flank of the Eighth Army, destroying the already shaky ROK II Corps in a matter of hours, leaving the Eighth Army's flank completely exposed. Capitalizing on the situation, the Chinese pushed ahead, hitting the 2nd Infantry Division with a massive attack. Their goal was to push to the coast and cut off the Eighth Army's retreat. The 2nd fought back hard, but against the hordes of Chinese troops they had little chance to standing their ground. The Division fell back, dogged at every step by the Chinese. In an effort to plug the gap Walker connected his reserves, the Turkish Brigade and the 1st Cavalry Division, but to no avail. There was no way to stop the estimated 200,000 Chinese. Within two days the Eighth Army was in full retreat. By 5 December it had abandoned the capital of Pyongyang and had out-distanced the pursuing enemy, who were slowed down by their lack of vehicles. By mid-December the army had set up defensive positions along the 38th Parallel and awaited the onslaught of the Chinese. Most of the army had managed to retire in good order due to the 2nd Infantry Division bearing the brunt of the Chinese assault. It lost 4000 men, but allowed the rest of the Eighth Army to pull out of the trap. The division was so decimated from this fighting that when the remnants reached safety it was declared combat ineffective.

In the east the Chinese threw seven divisions against the 1st Marine Division, strung out along the road to the Chosin Reservoir. The Chinese planned to overrun the Marines and drive to the coast. When this goal was achieved the majority of X Corps would be cut off and then could be defeated in detail. Fortunately the Marines had prepared for such an eventuality and were not caught off guard. The Division was, however, cut off and its major components at Yudam-ni, Hagaru, and Coto-ri were isolated from each other. Task Force Drysdale, a relief force of British and American Marines, and a few tanks managed to break through the Chinese lines and get through to Hagaru but only after suffering over sixty percent casualties. To the east, Task Force Faith, from the 7th Infantry Division, also tried to fight its way to Hagaru. With only M-16 halftracks and M-19 motor carriages for support, the unit fought through Chinese roadblocks until it was within five miles of the Marine lines when the commander was killed and the unit fell apart. Many men were captured but a few managed to make it to the Marine lines. Realizing the futility of such relief efforts the Marines prepared to fight their way south. Backed by Naval and Marine air support, the regiments at Yudam-ui fought their way through the Chinese to Hagaru on 6 December. From there they continued on to Koto-ri, fighting all the way. Tanks proved instrumental in delivering direct fire on roadblocks and hilltop positions. At night they provided much needed firepower as the Chinese attempted to storm the Marines' defensive positions under the cover of darkness. Once at Koto-ri, only a short distance remained before safety. However, a huge bridge had been destroyed and unless replacement sections could be flown in, the division's retreat was at an end. The fortunes of war smiled on the Leathernecks when the Air Force was able to parachute in whole bridge spans. The bridge was rebuilt, allowing the division to make it safely to Haungnam, where it was evacuated by sea.

During their withdrawal the Marines lost nearly 8000 men but had inflicted over 37,000 casualties on the enemy. These losses were so severe that the Chinese Ninth Army was unable to carry out any major attacks against the remainder of X Corps as it retreated to Hungnam. The entire Corps, behind naval and air support, was able to pull out through the port with little enemy interference. X Corps brought out all of its heavy equipment and whatever supplies were necessary. That which was deemed superfluous was destroyed to prevent it falling into enemy hands. This orderly evacuation was possible only because of the gallant withdrawal from Chosin Reservoir of the 1st Marine Division. Had the Marines been destroyed, it is doubtful that much of X Corps could have been saved. As it turned out the Chinese suffered a major defeat and the UN forces were able to retire in good order. By Christmas Day, the evacuation was completed and all port facilities and installations of value to the enemy were destroyed. The various units of X corps were taken by sea to southern Korea, where after a short rest and refitting period, they were once more committed to the fighting.

*see map 5

M-41 self-propelled 155mm howitzers fire on enemy positions north of Hamhung in support of the 7th Infantry Division. The vehicles are from the 92nd Field Artillery Battalion. The M-41 was based on the chassis of the M-24 light tank, as was the M-19. (US Army)

In November the first British Centurion tanks, from the 8th King's Royal Irish Hussars, landed at Inchon and moved north by train. They were unloaded at the North Korean capital of Pyongyang but before they could get into action the Chinese intervention forced UN forces to retreat from North Korea. Here a Centurion sits in the streets of the capital providing cover for retreating American forces. (US Army)

THE EARLY WEEKS

ROK M-3 halftrack in Chonan, July, 1950.

M4A3E8, 89th Tank Battalion, in support of the 5th Infantry Regiment near Haktong-ni, 28 August 1950.

The Bouncing BITCH

T-34 of the 109th Tank Regiment, 105th NKPA Tank Brigade, attached to the 3rd NKPA Infantry Division, near Chonui, July, 1950.

237

M-16 of the 92nd Anti-aircraft Battalion, 1st Cavalry, outside Tabu Dong, September, 1950.
Page 36

OLD EXPENDABLE

33

To keep engines from freezing tankers were forced to start their engines every few hours. The crews of these M-4s warm up their tanks prior to the withdrawal from Koto-ri, on 8 December. During the advance to the reservoir area M-4s were the only tanks able to move up with the Marines until the roads could be widened for the M-26s. (USMC)

(Left) With the onset of winter the temperature dropped sharply and icy road conditions made vehicle movement nearly impossible. The M-4 in the foreground slid off the road and is stuck in the ditch. Both tanks are armed with a 105mm howitzer and have had their dozer blades removed. (USMC)

As the withdrawal from the reservoir area continued, the town of Hungnam became a focal point for the evacuation of UN forces. Ringed by ground units and backed up by naval gunfire and air support, the town provided a haven for retreating units. This crew of an M-19 puts the finishing touches on their emplacement with straw to provide camouflage and a windbreak against the biting cold. (US Army)

Men of the 1st Marine Division board LVTs after their heroic thirteen-day fight out of a massive Chinese ambush. They will be taken by LVTs to troop transports in Hungnam Harbor. (USMC)

(Right) A South Korean SU-76 moves down the beach to a waiting LST for evacuation from Hungnam. Though used in the early stages of the war by ROK armored units, spare parts and ammunition supplies soon made it unfeasible to operate the Russian equipment and they were replaced with US vehicles. (US Army)

After their withdrawal from the Chosin Reservoir the 1st Marine Division was redeployed to the Marsan area to rest and rebuild its battle-weary units. However, even this far behind the lines, the Marines had to be on constant alert against guerrilla bands which had formed after the North Koreans had been pushed back north. This Pershing from the 1st Marine Tank Battalion covers a road near the Divisional Command Post on the outskirts of the city. (USMC)

THE PUSAN PERIMETER

Reworked M4A3 of A Company, 89th Tank Battalion, with units of the 29th Infantry Regiment, August, 1950.

M-26 Pershing, 1st Marine Brigade, 1st Tank Battalion, Company A, during the battle of the Naktong Bulge. This M-26 has received credit for three T-34 kills.

An Su-76, of the 2nd NKPA Infantry Division, captured near Changnyong by elements of the 23rd Infantry Regiment, September, 1950.

Marine M4(105)HVSS dozer pushes a T-34 off the road after the first battle of the Naktong Bulge, 17 August 1950.

INCHON AND THE BREAKOUT

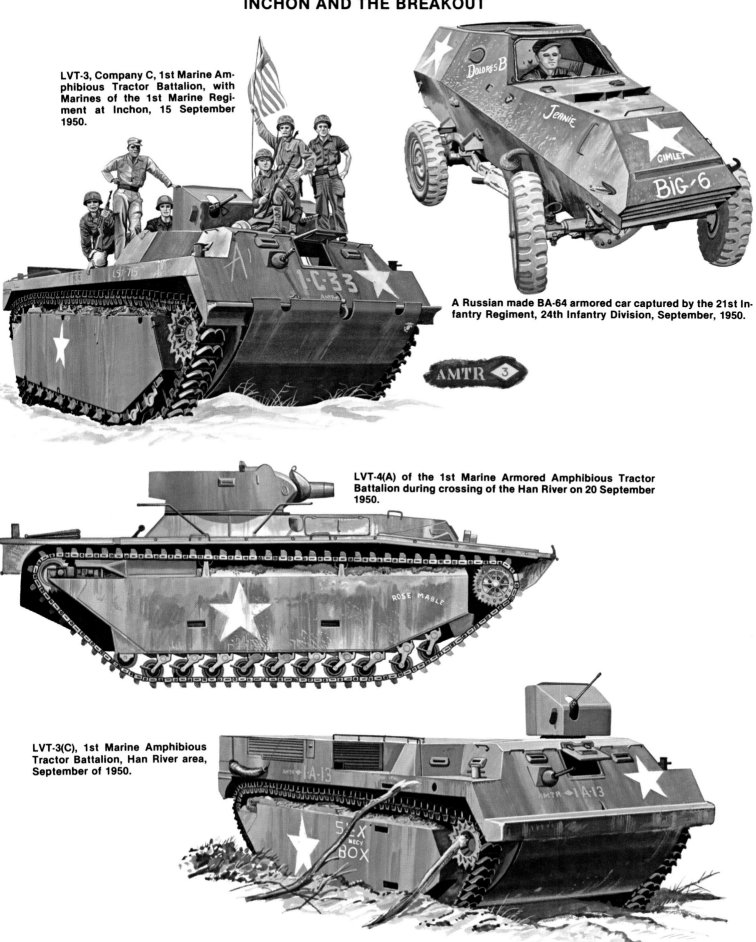

LVT-3, Company C, 1st Marine Amphibious Tractor Battalion, with Marines of the 1st Marine Regiment at Inchon, 15 September 1950.

A Russian made BA-64 armored car captured by the 21st Infantry Regiment, 24th Infantry Division, September, 1950.

LVT-4(A) of the 1st Marine Armored Amphibious Tractor Battalion during crossing of the Han River on 20 September 1950.

LVT-3(C), 1st Marine Amphibious Tractor Battalion, Han River area, September of 1950.

ATTACK AND COUNTERATTACK

By the end of December, the Eighth Army was dug in along the 38th Parallel, awaiting the Chinese offensive. During the retreat, General Walker had been killed in a jeep accident. To replace him, the Joint Chiefs of Staff selected General Matthew Ridgeway, the famous World War Two commander of the 82nd Airborne Division. Ridgeway arrived in Korea during the last week in December and tried to raise the low spirits of his men. Disdainful of all the talk of further retreat, Ridgeway tried to instill new fighting spirit in the Eighth Army. Unfortunately the Chinese did not give him much time. On New Year's Day, 1951, they launched a massive offensive along the front. Ridgeway tried to hold the ground until tank-led reinforcements and air support could relieve the threatened positions. However, the strength and ferocity of the Chinese attacks made it impossible to hold the line and Ridgeway ordered a gradual retirement. Covered by tanks and self-propelled anti-aircraft vehicles, most units were able to withdraw in good order. Unable to hold north of the Han River, Seoul was again abandoned and the Eighth Army crossed to the south side of the waterway. Ridgeway watched as the last armored vehicles, US self-propelled M-40s and British Centurions, crossed over the pontoon bridge.

These Centurion tanks, from the 8th King's Royal Irish Hussars (KRIH), had arrived at Pusan in mid-November. The regiment reached Pyongyang by train just as the Chinese launched their second offensive. Before the regiment even saw the enemy they were ordered to retreat. Throughout the long march back to the Parallel they had been forced to bypass most of the bridges because of the Centurion's 50-ton weight. As they forded the various rivers the massive tanks became coated with sheets of ice, chilling the crews to the bone. The regiment retreated in good order, despite the terrible conditions, and set up defensive positions south of the Han. From these positions the Centurions fired their guns in anger for the first time while supporting an American patrol along the Han. "Caughao", a Centurion from C Squadron, Headquarters Troop, came under fire from a Cromwell tank which the Chinese had captured. Along with another Centurion, fire was returned at a range of 3000 yards. The Cromwell was destroyed with the second shot, a rather remarkable feat of gunnery considering the range.

Following the initial impetus of the Chinese attack, their drive lost power. By mid-January the offensive had been stopped and the front stabilized along a line running between Pyongtaek and Samchok. Suspecting that the Chinese had lost the initiative Ridgeway sent the 27th Infantry Regiment, "The Wolfhounds", on a reconnaissance mission toward Osan. Supported by tanks, artillery and engineers the force reached the city without encountering significant resistance. The next day it reached Suwon before it ran into enemy troops. The regiment received orders to fall back since it had confirmed what Ridgeway suspected—that there were few Chinese troops in front of the Eighth Army. Eager to regain the initiative he ordered his troops to carry out harassing attacks on the Chinese, who were bringing up supplies and men in preparation for a new offensive. Ridgeway personally reconnoitered the front lines in an observation plane to remove any doubts in his own mind that the Chinese were lying low. Convinced the Chinese were not setting a trap for his troops, Ridgeway ordered the Eighth Army to attack on January 25th.

Seven columns, led by tanks, moved northward along the western edge of the battle zone. By early February they had reached the Han and had recaptured Inchon and Kimpo airfield. At first enemy resistance was light as the Chinese probed for a weak spot. This spot turned up in the center sector where the advancing forces were fragmented into five separate columns by the mountainous terrain. A mixed force of Chinese and North Koreans hit the US 2nd and ROK 8th Infantry Divisions. The 2nd was severely mauled while the 8th was all but annihilated, causing a general retreat in the sector which threatened the flank of the western drive.

The Chinese launched their main counterattack toward Chipyong-ni, midway between the western and central sectors. If they could achieve a breakthrough here the entire UN offensive would be placed in jeopardy. Defending the town was the 23rd Regimental Combat Team supported by tanks, several artillery batteries and a battery from the 82nd Anti-aircraft Battalion. This battery included six M-16s and four M-19s which were sited at various points around the perimeter. Following a direct order from Ridgeway not to withdraw, the unit dug in to await the Chinese onslaught. By February 13th their position was completely surrounded by three Chinese divisions. That night the enemy launched the first in a series of attacks against the regiment's perimeter. For three days the Red Chinese hammered at the encircled regiment. Within the position tanks and anti-aircraft vehicles moved about supporting the embattled infantrymen and leading counterattacks. Completely cut off, the defenders were resupplied air. In an effort to break through the encircling Chinese, the 1st Cavalry sent a relief force to open the road and reinforce the defenses of the position. The relief force was composed of the 5th Cavalry Regiment supported by a tank company (M-46s), two tank platoons (M-4s), a battalion of self-propelled howitzers, and various other support units. The force moved out during the night of 14 February, getting about halfway to Chipyong-ni before being halted by a destroyed bridge. After bridge repairs were made the unit moved out the next morning at daylight, but immediately ran into stiff resistance. The commander, realizing that only an armored force had a chance of breaking through to the beleagured regiment, ordered all his tanks to form a column for a dash through the Chinese lines. To protect the tanks from close-in infantry attacks a company of infantry was assigned to ride atop the tanks to provide support. This column, named Task Force Crombez, started out in the early afternoon of February 15th. Throughout the remainder of the day it fought its way along the narrow road, constantly under enemy fire. Chinese troops with bazookas, satchel charges, and even bangalore torpedos, tried to get close enough to the column to destroy or disable the tanks. Tank and infantry fire

Cromwell tanks from the reconnaissance troop of the 8th King's Royal Irish Hussars pass under a sign of thanks in Seoul as they withdraw from the capital during the Chinese counterattack against the 8th Army in December of 1950. This unit supported the 29th British Brigade during the retreat to positions south of Seoul. (US Army)

took a terrible toll of the attackers, and no tanks were initially lost. However, just outside Chipyong-ni the road passed through a narrow ravine, where the Chinese made an all-out effort to stop the force. One M-46 was destroyed at this last obstacle but the remainder of the tanks broke the Chinese position and were met by four tanks from Chipyong-ni. The entire force made its way back into the perimeter. Though low on ammunition, the arrival of Task Force Corombez did much to raise the morale of the defenders of the town. Moving into positions around the perimeter, the tanks spent an uneventful night in their new quarters. The next day the tanks returned to the main relief force without encountering enemy resistance, and escorted a resupply convoy back to the town. The siege was ended and with it the immediate danger to the UN offensive.

After the failure of the Chinese counterattack Ridgeway decided to keep up the pressure. Less then a week after the siege of Chipyong-ni was lifted, he ordered his forces to attack the battered enemy troops. OPERATION KILLER began on 21 February and was, as the name implies, designed to inflict maximum casualties on the Chinese with minimum UN casualties. Throughout the operation great emphasis was placed on air strikes, artillery support, and direct fire from tanks and anti-aircraft vehicles. Thousands of Chinese soldiers were killed as UN forces pushed relentlessly forward. By the end of February the communists had retreated back across the Han River. An early spring thaw caused extensive flooding and muddy conditions hampered the advancing forces. By the beginning of March a halt was called in the offensive to allow the troops to rest and be resupplied.

On 7 March Ridgeway launched Operation "Ripper", a two-pronged attack in the center of the UN lines. An unusual feature of this offensive was the gaudy paint schemes which many of the tanks carried. Intelligence had informed the various tank units that the Chinese were superstitious of tigers and dragons. To take advantage of this, many tank units painted faces of these animals on the fronts of their tanks and, in some cases, covered the entire vehicle with "tiger" stripes. Whether or not these schemes had any effect on the enemy is not known but it did raise morale and provided some of the most colorful armored schemes ever seen. But if the painted faces failed to make an impression on the Chinese, the various tank-infantry task forces with artillery and air support did. Throughout March "Ripper" pressed forward relentlessly. By the middle of the month, UN forces had crossed the Han and were back in Seoul. Communist forces, composed mostly of infantry, were unable to seriously hamper the Eighth Army. They broke contact and retreated as quickly as possible. In an effort to trap some of the retreating enemy troops north of Seoul the 187th Regimental Combat Team was airdropped into a blocking position along the Seoul-Kaesong highway. An armored task force was sent to link up with them, but the Chinese managed to avoid the trap and escaped. All along the front, resistance was light as

the various corps pushed northward again. By the first week in April the attacking forces had pushed back over the 38th Parallel into North Korea. Again unseasonal rains and the need to resupply slowed the offensive.

Then, suddenly, came the unbelievable. MacArthur was relieved! President Truman, unable to accept certain views and statements which MacArthur expressed, had decided to relieve him. Unfortunately the proud old general learned of this action through a news bulletin rather then a formal military message, a very cruel and heartless way to treat such a remarkable man with so distinguished a career. The President chose a capable replacement for him; General Ridgeway was ordered to take over MacArthur's command, and General James Van Fleet took over leadership of the Eighth Army. This changeover took place just as Operation "Ripper" was winding down. Ridgeway had hoped to keep the enemy off balance and unable to organize a new offensive but this hope was to no avail. In less than two weeks Van Fleet faced a new Chinese offensive which hoped to destroy the UN force.

The crew of this Daimler Dingo Mark II armored car await orders to move out during the retreat from Seoul. The vehicle is from the 8th King's Royal Irish Hussars. (US Army)

A Centaur dozer tank prepares a defensive position on the south side of the Han River after UN forces abandoned the northern bank to the Red Chinese. Unfortunately, this move still did not allow UN troops time to regroup, and they were forced to retreat still further south before the line was stabilized. (US Army)

TIGER TANKS

M-24 Chaffee from the 79th Tank Battalion in support of the 25th Infantry Division during OPERATION RIPPER, March, 1951.

M-46, 73rd Tank Battalion, OPERATION RIPPER, March, 1951.

M4A3E8, 64th Tank Battalion, attached to the 3rd Infantry Division, near Sokchon-ni, March, 1951.

M4A3E8, 65th Regimental Combat Team, 3rd Infantry Division during March of 1951.

SELF PROPELLED GUNS

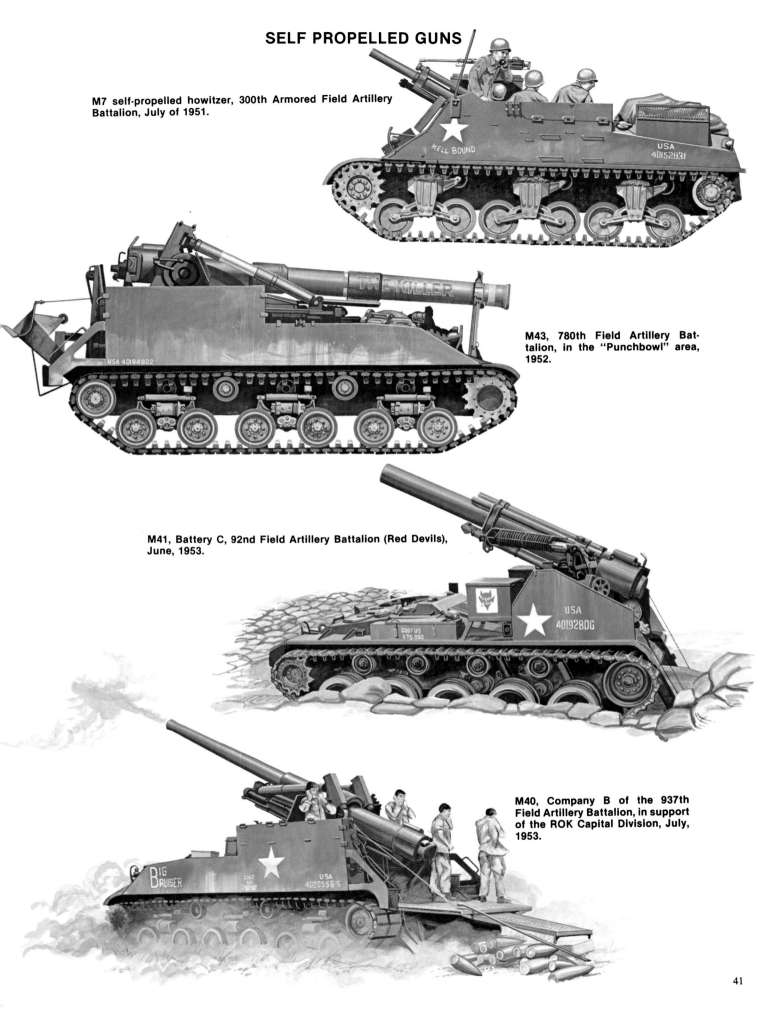

M7 self-propelled howitzer, 300th Armored Field Artillery Battalion, July of 1951.

M43, 780th Field Artillery Battalion, in the "Punchbowl" area, 1952.

M41, Battery C, 92nd Field Artillery Battalion (Red Devils), June, 1953.

M40, Company B of the 937th Field Artillery Battalion, in support of the ROK Capital Division, July, 1953.

This Centurion moves into a recently dug position scooped out by the Centaur dozer at the right. The Centurion proved to be a robust vehicle in combat and could often climb slopes which American tanks found exceedingly difficult or impossible. (US Army)

"Columbo", a Centurion Mk 3 from the 8th King's Royal Irish Hussars, moves up to defensive positions on the Han River near Seoul. It is marked with a US star for recognition and a removable plate on the side skirts, which bears a tactical identification. Centurions sometimes carried fuel drums on the rear deck because of supply difficulties. (US Army)

In addition to Centurions, British forces also brought Cromwell tanks with them. These were assigned to the Reconnaissance Troop of the 8th Hussars, and it was against a captured Cromwell that the Centurion engaged in its first tank vs tank action. (US Army)

(Above) The crew of this M-19 watches the town of Chamsil-li burn during the retreat following the Chinese offensive which began on New Year's Day, 1951. In an effort to slow the enemy down and deny him cover, UN troops were at times forced to follow a scorched-earth policy. Notice the Korean flag flying from this vehicle which was attached to the 3rd Infantry Division. (US Army)

(Below Left) An M-24 from the 73rd Tank Battalion, 7th Infantry Division, sits in the town of Sochon-ni while the crew awaits orders to move out. The tank was part of a reconnaissance patrol which was trying to locate Chinese units in pursuit of retreating UN forces. (US Army)

(Below) The crews of these armored jeeps prepare to go on patrol. Attempts to add armor to the lightweight jeep proved of little value since the vehicles were not powerful enough to carry the amount of armor needed to provide sufficient protection. These jeeps are from the intelligence and reconnaissance platoons of the 38th Infantry Regiment, 2nd Division. (US Army)

ALLIED ARMOR

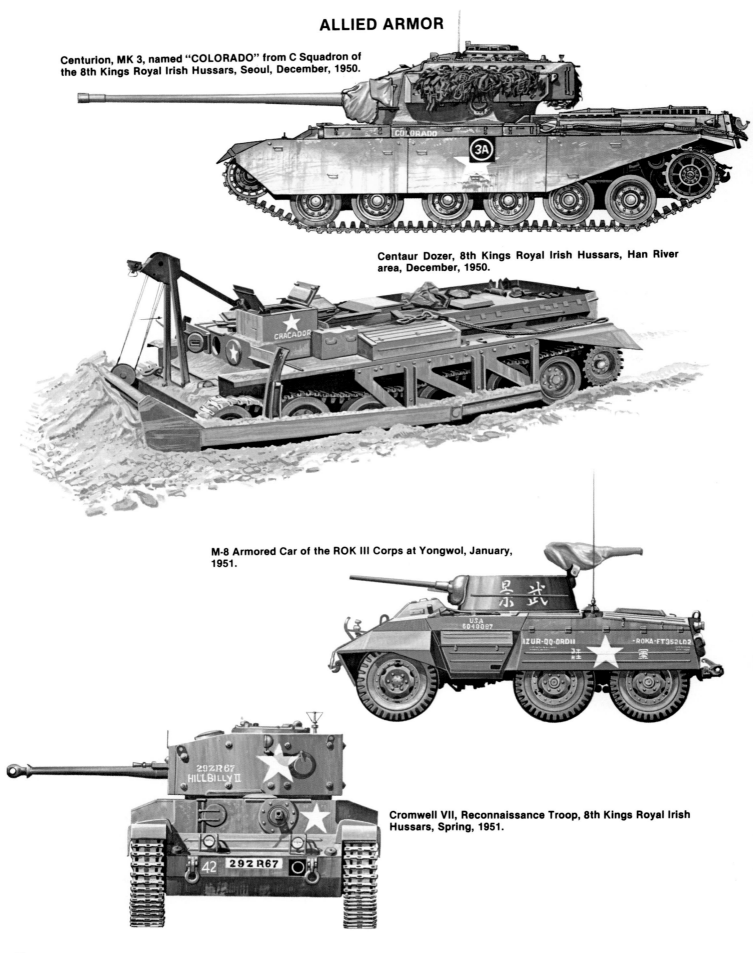

Centurion, MK 3, named "COLORADO" from C Squadron of the 8th Kings Royal Irish Hussars, Seoul, December, 1950.

Centaur Dozer, 8th Kings Royal Irish Hussars, Han River area, December, 1950.

M-8 Armored Car of the ROK III Corps at Yongwol, January, 1951.

Cromwell VII, Reconnaissance Troop, 8th Kings Royal Irish Hussars, Spring, 1951.

M4A3 Dozer, "CUDDLES", C Squadron, Lord Strachcona's Horse, Autumn, 1951.

Australian Pattern Carrier MK 2, Summer, 1952.

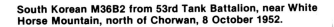

South Korean M36B2 from 53rd Tank Battalion, near White Horse Mountain, north of Chorwan, 8 October 1952.

Korean M-24 Chaffee, Korean Training Center, Summer, 1953.

This Marine patrol fires on enemy guerrillas in the Pohang area of South Korea. These "rice paddy patrols" were often supported by armor such as these M-26s and M-4s, which gave the leathernecks all the firepower they needed. Note the different positioning of the company markings on the three tanks. (USMC)

This M-4 and M-16 from the 72nd Tank Battalion were destroyed during a Chinese attack on a column of the 2nd Infantry Division in February. The area was later retaken by units of the 1st Marine Division. (USMC)

The crew of this M-16 "Betty" fires on Chinese troops during a probe by elements of the 27th Infantry Regiment, of the 25th Infantry Division, in the Seoul area in February of 1951. (US Army)

(Left) During the UN counter attack a bit of psychological warfare was tried on the Chinese, who were supposedly very superstitious about cats or dragons. Many tank units painted fierce faces on the fronts of their tanks to instill fear into the enemy. Whether or not this worked is unknown but it did improve the troops' morale, and fit into the general aggressive behavior which the new Eighth Army commander, General Ridgeway, was trying to foster. (US Army)

A Daimler Armored Car and Dingo Scout Car from the 8th Hussars in early 1951. As the war progressed, a good deal of American equipment was substituted in Commonwealth formations to ease supply problems. (Dunstan)

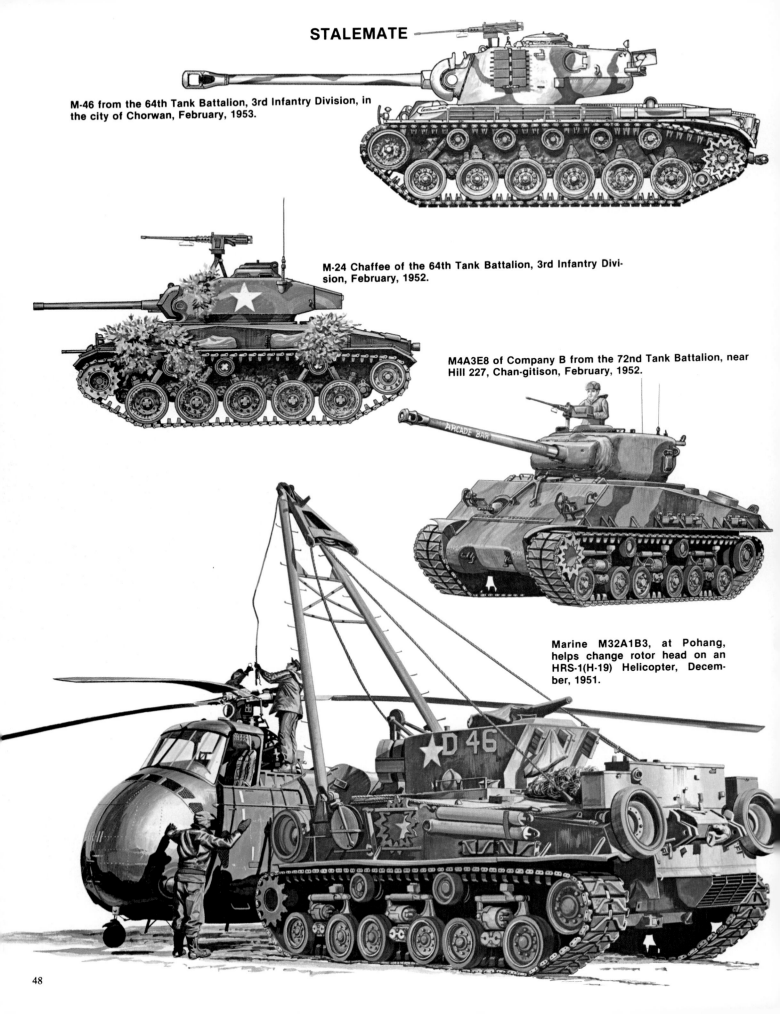

STALEMATE

M-46 from the 64th Tank Battalion, 3rd Infantry Division, in the city of Chorwan, February, 1953.

M-24 Chaffee of the 64th Tank Battalion, 3rd Infantry Division, February, 1952.

M4A3E8 of Company B from the 72nd Tank Battalion, near Hill 227, Chan-gitison, February, 1952.

Marine M32A1B3, at Pohang, helps change rotor head on an HRS-1(H-19) Helicopter, December, 1951.

A variety of tractors, trucks, trailers and armored cars from the New Zealand Artillery Battalion move up to the front from their reserve positions at Pusan following the start of the UN offensive. Though the support of the UN member Nations was welcomed, the diversity of their equipment created logistical nightmares. (US Army)

(Right) A Sherman tank with a cat face carries troops of the 1st Cavalry in pursuit of retreating Chinese forces in the vicinity of Chi-pyong. The tank is believed to be from the 70th Tank Battalion. (US Army)

A Churchill bridgelayer removes a temporary span after the bridge in the background has been repaired. The British inclusion of such vehicles in their armored units stemmed from their experience in World War Two. The British were pioneers in adapting armored vehicles to such unusual tasks. (US Army)

These M-4s carry one of the most unusual schemes applied to any tanks during the "cat" period. The fronts of the tanks were painted Tan, then hundreds of hand-painted Green squiggles were added to serve as a base for the leering mouths. The tanks are from the 89th Tank Battalion of the 25th Infantry Division. (US Army)

This Sherman from the 64th Tank Battalion, 3rd Infantry Division, got bogged down in the Han River and had to be towed out. From the ice on the track guard it appears the tank did not get stuck in water too deep. The cat's head is superimposed on the division's shoulder patch. (US Army)

An M4A3 dozer tank from the 3rd Engineer Battalion, 24th Infantry Division, sits on a road on the outskirts of Seoul. This tank is equipped with the old style suspension. The pattern on the hull is Tan over Olive drab. (US Army)

A platoon of M-46 Pattons from the 6th Tank Battalion, 24th Infantry Division, line up in firing positions facing Chinese lines. Besides the normal .50 caliber machinegun carried on the turret, the crews of the two closest tanks have mounted an additional .30 caliber weapon on the rear of the turret. (US Army)

A column of M-4s from C Company, 89th Tank Battalion, of the 25th Infantry Division, move north after crossing the Han River in March. The tanks of this unit carried the name "RICE'S RED DEVILS" on their turrets and a devil motif on the frontal armor. Rice was the company commander's last name. (US Army)

One of the "RED DEVILS" advances across a rocky field near the Han River. (US Army)

(Above) This tiger head adorns the front of an M-46 from the 73rd Tank Battalion of the 7th Infantry Division. Note how the side flaps have been raised to provide additional storage. (US Army)

(Below Left) An M15A1 of the Turkish Brigade sits in a prepared position along the front in the early spring of 1951. The brigade was often used as a corps reserve and committed to "hot spots" as the need arose. It acquired a reputation as an outstanding fighting unit. (US Army)

The crew of this M-16 prepares to fire on Chinese positions north of Chae-jae. The volume of fire thrown out by the quad .50 could literally sweep a position clean unless enemy troops were under heavy cover. However, such a volume of fire used up tremendous quantities of ammunition and wore the machinegun barrels out at an alarming rate unless they were given time to cool down. (US Army)

This M-7 has been modified to permit high-angle firing because the steep Korean hills severely restricted the area the old gun mounts could put under fire. (US Army)

In an effort to provide the crews of M-16s with more protection, a new shield was developed for the gun mount. The new shield was designed by the 702nd Ordnance Company of the 2nd Infantry Division. (US Army)

An M-24 moves slowly down a steep slope southeast of Kaesong as it supports troops of the 25th Infantry Division as they push toward the 38th Parallel. Believed to be from the 89th Tank Battalion, the turret-mounted .50 caliber machinegun has been replaced by a .30 caliber machinegun. A camouflage pattern, or possibly a cat's head, has been painted on the gun mantlet. (US Army)

An M-24, with the remains of a cat head on its front armor plate, advances along a road in the area around Seoul. Since most crews climbed aboard their tanks on the front armor plate, these heads were soon worn off and few crews had either the time or paint to redo them. (US Army)

This gaudily painted M-46 helps pull out a sister tank mired in the mud near the town of Chongpyong. The primitive road network in Korea made difficult going, even for tracked vehicles, particularly when they became muddy. These tanks are from the 6th Battalion of the 24th Infantry Division. (US Army)

(Above) Even the relatively light M-24 could cause the primitive Korean roads to collapse. This tank from the 24th Reconnaissance Company, 24th Infantry Division, sits in a ditch after the shoulder of the road gave away under it. Because of the cramped interior of the M-24 the crew was forced to carry most items of personnel gear on the outside of the tank. (US Army)

The crew of this M-3 halftrack fire on enemy positions near Yangu. The M-3 did not see widespread service in Korea other than with anti-aircraft artillery battalions, and was often used as a mobile fire base due to the number of machineguns it could carry. This vehicle is from the 15th Anti-aircraft Battalion. (US Army)

These Marines await a tow in an army DUKW which bogged down in the Pukhan River during the 8th Army's spring offensive against the Chinese. From their looks, the Marines' opinion of their army transport does not appear too high. (USMC)

(Below) These M-37s fire on Chinese troops north of the Han River. The M-37 was based on the M-24 chassis and carried a 105mm howitzer. It was designed to replace the older M-7 Priest. (US Army)

THE FRONT STABILIZES

In response to OPERATION RIPPER the communists launched a massive three-pronged offensive with over 350,000 men on the night of 23 April. Two secondary attacks were carried out in the center and eastern sections of the Eighth Army's front line but the main effort was directed in the western sector. The Chinese hit the UN line with an enveloping attack aimed at isolating and eventually recapturing Seoul. Directly in the path of this thrust sat the 29th British Brigade along the Imjin River. The enemy struck in overwhelming numbers and isolated the Gloucester and Belgium battalions of the brigade. In an effort to stop the Chinese and rescue these forces, Centurions from the 8th Hussars (KRIH), along with the Fusilier and Ulster Battalions, tried to fight their way to the surrounded units. Unfortunately, the Chinese were in such strength that the effort bogged down. That night the Belgium battalion escaped but the Gloucesters were unable to break out. A second attempt was made the next day with the help of a Filipino battalion backed up by M-24s, but this also failed. Additional enemy pressure threatened to cut off the relieving forces, which were then ordered to retire. Covered by the Centurions, the Fusiliers and Ulsters pulled back under heavy enemy fire. Throughout the retreat the Centurions kept the Chinese from overrunning the battalions. At times enemy troops were climbing atop the Centurions with grenades and sticky bombs, but the tanks raked each other with machine-gun fire, sweeping the Chinese off. By the end of the day the remnants of the battalions, covered by Centurions, were able to reach safety. Unfortunately the Gloucester Battalion, surrounded, low on food, water and ammunition, could not break out. The battalion was forced to surrender after putting up a heroic resistance. Despite losing over a quarter of its strength the brigade inflicted heavy casualties on the Chinese, seriously hampering their effectiveness. Had it not been for the outstanding support of the Centurions, the unit would probably have been overrun and the Chinese might have turned the UN flank.

Although the Chinese were able to breech the UN line in the center, the bulk of the line held. To keep from having his units outflanked, Van Fleet ordered a gradual withdrawal while tank and artillery fire kept the communists at bay. The Chinese found it difficult to counter this as they had neither armor nor artillery to match the Eighth Army. By the end of April the enemy offensive slowed to a crawl as UN forces fell back to prepared positions just north of Seoul. As the Chinese halted to regroup, Van Fleet sent out patrols; armored units probed up to tén miles in front of the UN lines without serious opposition. Van Fleet ordered a limited counterattack to regain some of the lost ground, but as enemy resistance stiffened his units were ordered to dig in and brace for a new Chinese offensive.

This new offensive was launched on the night of 15 May, when thirty enemy divisions were thrown against the UN lines. The main thrust occurred in the center and east sectors where twenty-one Chinese divisions broke through the front. However, the units on the flanks of the breakthrough bent their lines back to contain the Chinese attack rather than retreat. Forces were rushed into the breech with tank and artillery support to seal holes in the line. Again, the Chinese were unable to exploit their initial victory and by 20 May their drive had ground to a halt. Van Fleet seized this opportunity to launch a counterattack along the whole front. Led by armor, UN forces drove the Chinese back across the 38th Parallel and regained much of the ground which had been captured in OPERATIONS KILLER and RIPPER. However, an order from the Joint Chiefs of Staff forced the Eighth Army to halt. Although Van Fleet was allowed enough latitude to launch local attacks, to gain better defensive positions he was instructed not to push deeply into North Korea. This order came from Washington; unknown to the soldiers in the field a new phase of the war was about to set in—a phase that would last for over two frustrating years, and deny UN forces the final victory for which they had shed so much blood.

This lineup of M-24s belongs to the 187th Airborne Regimental Combat Team. This airborne unit became the first such unit to have tanks assigned to it as part of its organic strength. The 187th made few parachute drops during the war, but was usually assigned as a reserve to the theater commander. (US Army)

An M-39 leads a column of M-7 Priests toward the central front of the UN lines in April of 1951. The self-propelled guns are on their way to relieve the artillery elements of the 1st Marine Division.

"CAROL LEE", an M16 assigned to the 17th Regimental Combat Team of the 7th Infantry Division, fires on an enemy hilltop position near Munye-ri as infantry move into position for an assault. Barbed wire is carried on the front fender for use when the crew set up their night positions. (US Army)

(Left) The crew of this M-3 APC keep a careful eye on a load of Korean refugees which they are transporting to a relocation center. Oftentimes the communists tried to slip soldiers in with the refugees, who would try to kill unwary UN soldiers. The halftrack is from the 7th Reconnaissance Company, 7th Infantry Division. (US Army)

Two Achilles self-propelled guns from the 25th Canadian Infantry Brigade sit on the docks in Pusan after being unloaded from a cargo ship. Although deployed with the Canadian Brigade these vehicles were not used in combat, being replaced by M-4s. This was done to simplify logistical problems and because the M-4s were more suitable in the role of infantry support than the Achilles with its open fighting compartment.(Public Archives Canada PA via Storey).

Spring rains made the going tough even for tanks. This Sherman from the 65th Tank Company, 64th Tank Battalion, is bogged down in mud after it slid off a road. From the looks of the situation the only way the tank will get free is to be towed by another tank or tank retriever. (US Army)

The crew of this M-24 Chaffee fire on a group of Chinese during a patrol near the village of Songdong-bong. The tank, "Eagle Claw", is from the 3rd Reconnaissance Company of the 3rd Infantry Division. Once the threat of enemy T-34s had diminished, the Chaffee proved useful in the role of infantry support and scouting. Note the spent shells below the bogey wheels, and crewmen armed with M-1 rifles rather than the less effective standard issue M-1 carbine. (US Army)

This M-37 unit takes a break during the advance north of Seoul. They are from the 58th Armored Field Artillery Battalion of the 3rd Infantry Division. The 58th was an all Negro unit except for a few white officers; later in the war it was desegregated. (US Army)

During the retreat in early April M-26s were lost to enemy action. These vehicles were recovered when the area was recaptured by elements of the 24th Infantry Division. The Pershing on the right carries the striped tiger pattern on the turret. The Pershing on the left evidently caught fire, since the rubber in the tracks and bogey wheels has entirely burned off and the turret and hull are completely blackened. (US Army)

A mud spattered M-19 from the 3rd Anti-aircraft Battalion provides fire support to the 7th Regimental Combat Team of the 3rd Infantry Division. The M-19 could carry 336 rounds of 40mm ammunition in the turret storage bin along with whatever the crew stuffed into the interior spaces. The crew of this vehicle has mounted a .30 caliber machine gun on the front of the vehicle for their own close-in protection should the need arise. (US Army)

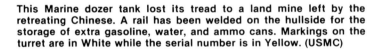

This Marine dozer tank lost its tread to a land mine left by the retreating Chinese. A rail has been welded on the hullside for the storage of extra gasoline, water, and ammo cans. Markings on the turret are in White while the serial number is in Yellow. (USMC)

A Marine Corps M-4 flamethrower heads up an armored column as it moves up to take part in a counterattack against the stalled Chinese spring offensive. Once the enemy drive was stopped, UN forces were able to push the Chinese back to the general area of the 38th Parallel. Both M-4s are carrying extra fuel drums on their rear decks. (USMC)

A Centurion from the 8th Hussars crosses a pontoon bridge over the Imjin River. Centurions from a number of different units played a decisive role in this sector as the Chinese attempted to seize hilltops, notably the "Hook", in order to turn the flank of Commonwealth troops holding the sector. (Dunstan)

Primitive conditions in Korea made maintenance a nightmare, with recovery vehicles proving to be invaluable when more permanent installations were not available. This M-32 lifts the turret off an M-46 at the 2nd Ordnance Heavy Weapons Repair Shop in Yongdongpo. The M-46 is from the 73rd Tank Battalion of the 3rd Infantry Division. (US Army)

British M-3s sit near the front in the spring of 1951. The middle one is obviously being used as an ambulance. When the Commonwealth units received American equipment it took them a while to remove the US markings. (Dunstan)

An M-39 of the 2nd Infantry Division carries a team of tactical air officers to the front on a spotting mission. The crew has added a tripod-mounted .30 caliber machinegun for additional protection against infantry. (US Army)

An M-7 self-propelled gun moves down a road past a column of troops from the 24th Infantry Division during a counterattack against the Chinese spring offensive. The M-7 is believed to be from Company D of the 8th Armored Battalion. Note the face tiger face on the mudguard. (US Army)

This M-7, "HELLBOUND" of the 300th Armored Field Artillery, has just fired a round at Chinese positions and the gun tube is in full recoil. (US Army)

With a load of ROKs aboard, this M-46 from the 73rd Tank Battalion prepares to cross the Imjin River to help secure a bridgehead. During the spring offensive the front fluctuated back and forth as both sides strove to gain the upper hand. Eventually UN forces were able to regain the initiative and push the Chinese back across the 38th Parallel. In the push back north the Imjin posed little in the way of a hindrance because of its relatively shallow depth. (US Army)

This M-4 Sherman had the distinction of being the oldest tank in the 72nd Tank Battalion. It is painted in the summer camouflage scheme of Earth Brown over Olive Drab, which was used by some tank units during the second summer of the war. The markings on the turret are small flags of all the UN countries which the battalion had supported to this date. (US Navy)

"AITA'S ANKIES", an M-40 self-propelled 155mm gun, fires on Chinese positions near Yanggu June of 1951. The vehicle is from the 937th Field Artillery Battalion and belongs to A Battery. Each battery had their vehicles marked with names using the battery's letter. (USArmy)

The crew of this "Wasp" flamethrower sends a stream of flame toward a practice target. This variant of the Universal Carrier was assigned to Princess Patricia's Canadian Light Infantry. These vehicles did not see front-line service due to their limited mobility in the steep Korean terrain and their lack of overhead protection for the crew. (Public Archives Canada via Storey)

To transport damaged or broken-down armor both the armored and unarmored version of the M-25 tank transporter were used by the various ordnance units. Both these vehicles are from the 57th Ordnance Recovery Company. (US Army)

STALEMATE

Despite the order to halt his offensive along the so-called "Kansas Line", just above the 38th Parallel, Van Fleet was authorized to carry out localized attacks. Selected units pushed forward to gain more favorable defensive positions while reserve troops strengthened the line against possible Chinese attacks. Throughout June elements of the Eighth Army kept pressure on communist lines. Led by tanks, the 1st Cavalry Division captured Chorwon despite spirited enemy resistance and numerous mine fields, and further east US and Turkish troops captured Kumhwa. Both these towns, along with Pyonggang, were part of a major enemy supply and communications center known as the "Iron Triangle". From these newly won positions two tank-infantry task forces set out for Pyonggang. Meeting only light resistance the two forces reached the city, only to find it deserted. However, they soon discovered that the enemy held the high ground north of the city in strength, and wisely decided to retire before being cut off. Other units also reported finding Chinese troop concentrations in the area, and from these reports it appeared that the communists were establishing their own frontline, a counterpart of the "Kansas Line". Before long the same pattern was being detected along the rest of the front. By mid-June Van Fleet was satisfied with the general results of his limited drives and large-scale attacks were discontinued. In their place various elements of the Eighth Army carried out small patrol actions and engaged in local fire-fights. Though these actions were sometimes intense, they did not materially affect the front line, which had been readjusted after the limited gains of early June.

Then, on 23 June 1951, the Soviet delegate to the United Nations proposed that truce talks be held between the two warring sides. Eager to bring an end to the war which had already cost over 80,000 American casualties, President Truman instructed General Ridgeway to open discussions with the communists. Unfortunately this move was based more on political considerations than the military situation. At this point in the war the North Korean Army had been almost completely destroyed after having lost over 600,000 men, killed, wounded, or taken prisoner. The Chinese had also suffered tremendous casualties, having lost over half a million men since they entered the war. Aside from a manpower edge the communists could not match the Eighth Army in strength—tanks, artillery, or supporting naval and air power. In addition Van Fleet had submitted a proposal whereby he planned to use the 1st Marine Division in a series of amphibious assaults to outflank the Chinese lines in order to produce the same effect as the Inchon landing. With the great mobility his forces enjoyed over the enemy, Van Fleet was certain he could quickly achieve a complete victory.

However, by this stage of the war the idea of complete victory, as espoused by MacArthur, had fallen into disfavor. Rather the theory of "limited war" had come into vogue. Under this philosophy, the administration rationalized that since South Korea had been cleared of enemy troops the risks of going for complete victory entailed too many pitfalls. A drive to the Yalu, aside from the casualties it could incur, would increase UN front line from 110 to 420 miles and would require a far greater number of US troops and financial support. In addition, there was the risk that Russia and China might become directly involved in the conflict (the Red Chinese had steadfastly maintained the fiction that those Chinese troops fighting in Korea were volunteers). The politicians in Washington decided that only limited goals were to be set for the field army and these goals would be based on political considerations.

Unfortunately, the acceptance of the communist offer to talk resulted in a stalemate which was to last over two years before a tenuous truce was signed.

During this period the enemy rebuilt his shattered formations and received huge stocks of Russian equipment, particularly artillery, which helped to put the enemy on a more equal footing with the Eighth Army. Due to political considerations the Eighth Army was hamstrung when it was overwhelmingly superior to the Chinese and North Koreans; the communists were allowed to rebuild their forces until a complete victory was nearly impossible to achieve. It became obvious that the only reason the Russians suggested the truce talks was that the Red Chinese were fast approaching the same threshold of disaster that the North Koreans had found themselves on. In this respect the proposal probably far exceeded even what the Russians had hoped for.

A good example of how the communists used the peace talks to their advantage can be found in the revitalization of their armored formations. By time the Chinese intervened in late 1950, North Korean armored units had all but ceased to exist, and the Chinese left all their tanks and self-propelled guns in Manchuria so as not to restrict their mobility in the mountainous Korean terrain. Throughout 1950 and the first half of 1951 the communists made no effort to employ their few armored vehicles except in minor roles. However, from July 1951, when the peace talks started they began to rebuild these shattered formations and bring in new units. By April 1952 the communists had on hand a full Chinese armored division, a full North Korean armored division, and a mechanized division, with a total strength of 520 T-34s and SU-76s.

Peace talks dragged on for two years, and fighting continued along the entire front for most of the two years. However, this fighting remained localized in nature and never again did either side carry out a full-scale offensive. Aside from some relatively minor changes, the positions of both sides were still the same when the war finally ended in the summer of 1953. Throughout these two years the front remained essentially stagnant, except for occasional forays to capture prisoners or gain slightly better defensive positions. Unfortunately, this led to a sort of military "King Of The Hill" game where each side fought a battle of wills over relatively worthless high ground. Names such as Baldy, Heartbreak Ridge, White Horse, and Pork Chop Hill were the sites of pitched battles, which served no other purpose than to cost further thousands of casualties, mostly Chinese and North Korean, but also UN casualties. For two years such positions were fought over and changed hands countless times as the truce talks dragged on. During this period the war took on aspects of the trench warfare carried on during World War One on the Western Front.

With the stabilization of the front armored units lost their mobility. During this phase tanks were often used in "bunker busting", infantry support, and occasionally as part of a raiding force. Of these uses "bunker busting" became the most frequent job in which armor came to be employed. Since each side fortified the high ground opposite one another, these positions provided a wide field of fire. Each side dug thousand of bunkers for crew-served weapons, observation posts, command posts and shelters for troops and vehicles. The flat trajectory of tank guns provided the best chance of destroying these Chinese and North Korean positions. Unfortunately, getting the tanks to the top of these steep hills was exceeding difficult at times. For this role the lighter weight and smaller size of the M-24 Chaffee or the M-4 Sherman were an asset compared to the heavier M-26 Pershing, M-46 Patton, and the Centurion. However, their lighter armament was not as effective as that of the heavier guns of the other medium tanks and they usually required more rounds to destroy bunkers.

An M-4 from the 72nd Tank Battalion fires on Chinese positions near Hill 227 during an attack by units of the 2nd Infantry Division. The tank is in the summer camouflage scheme of Earth over Olive Drab. (US Army)

Because the tanks were often silhouetted against the skyline when they took up their firing positions the enemy usually responded with an intense artillery or mortar barrage. Rarely were communist gunners able to score direct hits, although flying shrapnel often damaged treads, vision ports, antennas and other external fittings. All this shelling did little to endear the tanks to the infantry around them who would have preferred being left in peace. As soon as a particular firing mission was completed the tanks were withdrawn to another emplacement or pulled back to the rear. When the tanks were required to remain on-line for any length of time their emplacements were usually protected by sandbags, logs, or earthworks. If the area was subjected to major shelling the tanks were sometimes provided with an overhead cover of timber and sandbags. Many tank crews put layers of sandbags over the rear deck to protect the engine from a possible mortar shell.

From these hilltop emplacements the tanks also were able to support infantry raids or patrols against enemy positions. In preparation for such actions, which were normally carried out at night, the tankers registered their guns on possible targets during the day which were then coded. These codes were given to the infantry unit taking part in the action. If a raiding party needed support that night, the codes were called in and the tank's main armament could rapidly be brought to bear. Such timely support often saved a patrol from being trapped or decimated by enemy fire.

Self-propelled artillery and self-propelled anti-aircraft guns were also employed along the front in direct infantry support. The self-propelled artillery pieces were occasionally brought up to the front when a particular bunker or field fortification proved especially stubborn in resisting tank fire. Firing over open sights, these guns wrought tremendous destruction on the communist positions because of their accuracy and hitting power. Unfortunately, they were also prime targets for counter-artillery fire and could usually only get off a few rounds before they had to move. The self-propelled anti-aircraft vehicles, primarily the M-16 and M-19, while not able to offer the destructive power or range of tanks or artillery, could deliver a tremendous volume of fire on a target of intermediate range. Though both vehicles were open-topped and susceptible to enemy counter-battery fire, especially mortars, their accuracy allowed them to sweep exposed enemy positions clean. In particular, the M-16 with its four .50 caliber machine guns provided a high volume of fire which could decimate attacking waves of Chinese or North Korean infantry.

During this phase of the war a number of hill positions changed hands numerous times as both sides fought a war of wills. Usually these positions were too steep to allow tanks to accompany the infantry up the slopes. Tanks or self-propelled vehicles would move as far up the slopes as possible to provide supporting fire. The flat trajectory of their guns made them ideal for this job rather than artillery which was not nearly as accurate in this role. The vehicle's .50 caliber machine guns also proved particularly effective in keeping the enemy pinned down until the last few moments of an assault, and often allowed UN infantry to get close to the enemy with minimal casualties.

In these battles for hilltop positions tanks also played an instrumental role in their defense. A number of tanks were fitted with turret-mounted searchlights to improve their night-fighting capability. In one spectacular engagement Marine M-46s equipped with searchlights fought a night-long action in support of the Turkish Brigade. During the engagement over 700 Chinese were killed by the Turks, due mainly to the tanks' illumination of the battlefield and their firepower. Other actions, though less spectacular, were just as important. From late 1952 until the end of the war a bitter struggle was waged between the Chinese and the Commonwealth Division over a position which jutted into the Chinese lines. Nicknamed "The Hook", this position was subjected to enemy assault after assault. Had the position fallen, the division's flank would have been exposed and would have necessitated a

withdrawal. Throughout the defense of the position Centurions played an important part in "The Hook's" defense. On a number of occasions these heavy tanks supported the position with direct fire or actually crawled atop the hill to aid the defenders. In almost every case the presence of the Centurions was the prime reason why the position was either held or retaken.

On occasion tanks were also employed on raids which were carried out to capture prisoners or destroy important enemy positions along the front. During the fight for "Heartbreak Ridge" the North Koreans fought the 2nd Infantry Division to a standstill. In an effort to break the stalemate a path was cleared through the surrounding hills for Shermans of the 72nd Tank Battalion. Upon completion of the road Tank Company B broke through the front, outflanking the enemy on the ridge, cutting their supply line to Mundung-ni. For a week fighting raged over the hill but finally the enemy was forced off. During this period the tankers of B Company constantly moved back and forth along the road to Mundung-ni, disrupting enemy resupply efforts and troop movements. This kept the enemy so off-balance that no significant reinforcements could reach the ridge.

Other actions were not as successful. During OPERATION JEHU in June of 1952, two Centurion troops from the 5th Royal Inniskling Dragoon Guards took part in a successful raid on enemy positions at Point 156. In this action three tanks became bogged down and an armored recovery vehicle (ARV) was sent to retrieve them. This ARV ran over a mine and was disabled. A second ARV was sent to the scene but enemy shell fire cut its cable and wounded a crewman. A medical "Tug" (turretless Centurion) was then sent forward to evacuate the casualty but it also became bogged down. Thus by mid-afternoon five vehicles were bogged down in "no man's" land. Throughout the remainder of the day recovery efforts went on and by nightfall three of the vehicles had been recovered. The other two were finally recovered after several days of work but the total effort expended on these recoveries far outweighed the value of the raid. Further raids in this area were severely curtailed.

During a raid in the Kumwha Valley two M-4s were disabled by mines and abandoned. Rather than recover the tanks and risk casualties, both tanks were destroyed by other tanks in the section. When the report of the action was turned in, the corps commander was furious over the loss of two tanks. The divisional commander sent word to the regimental commander about how upset the Old Man was. The regimental commander, tongue in cheek, replied that there must have been a mistake and that the tanks were only disabled and would be turned in the next day. The regiment proceeded to retrieve the burned-out hulks, without casualties, shipping them back to the rear area the next day. Unfortunately, the comments from the rear area ordinance officer were not recorded.

Just before the final cease-fire the communists made one last bid to seize more ground, but they achieved little other than to cause additional bloodshed. After nearly two years of meaningless haggling the armistice was finally signed on 27 July 1953. But even after the signing of the cease-fire agreement fighting continued as the communists violated the truce with numerous incidents. To this day fighting still flares up along the border and the South Koreans must maintain large forces along the 38th parallel to insure its freedom. Both sides also maintain sizeable armored formations, and if full-scale warfare ever again breaks out on the Korean peninsula, tanks will play a vital part in it.

This M-39 struck a mine during a patrol near Chongyon-ni. The blast has torn off the tread, destroyed the drive sprocket and a bogey wheel. However, it appears that the hull of the vehicle is little the worse for wear and will probably be back in operation soon. (US Army)

An M-40 from Battery C of the 204th Field Artillery Battalion fires on enemy positions north of Yonchon in August, 1951. The dragon on the side is a rather unusual piece of artwork. Another unusual feature is the lack of serial numbers on the hull. (US Army)

(Left)The Air Force acquired a few M-20 armored cars for base security to counter attempts by the communists to use saboteurs against aircraft and ground installations. This armored car, still bearing its Army serial number, moves past an F-51 Mustang of the 18th Fighter Bomber Wing. The Air Police have added their own unit markings and cartoon to the hull. (USAF)

An M-7 of the 300th Field Artillery Battalion fires in support of the 1st Marine Division during fighting around Inji in central Korea. At this stage of the war enemy counter-battery fire was considered sufficient to warrant the use of camouflage netting and other deceptive devices. (US Army)

Once the attacks and counter-attacks of the spring and summer died down the front began to stabilize and over the next two years there was little change in the front lines. Both sides dug in and tanks lost their mobility, being used mainly as mobile pillboxes in hilltop positions. These Marine M-46s are being rearmed and refueled during a lull in the fighting. (USMC)

(Right) M-4s, still carrying their summer camouflage scheme, advance across frozen rice paddies toward Chinese positions on Hill 227 near Changitison. They are from Company B, 72nd Tank Battalion, 2nd Infantry Division. (US Army)

The job of guarding prisoners fell partially upon Army Military Police, which used a number of armored vehicles, including halftracks and armored cars. This M-8 belongs to the 556th Military Police Escort Guard of the 2nd Logistical Command. This unit had responsibility for guarding the POW compound at Pusan. Besides the American crew there is a Korean interpreter riding in the turret who can be distinguished by his dark helmet. (US Army)

As tanks were used more and more as mobile pillboxes, attempts were made to provide them with additional protection from enemy counter-battery fire. This M-4 has been partially dug in and surrounded by sandbags to give the tank's thinner side armor additional protection. (US Army)

(Left) An M-39 from the 2nd Infantry Division being used as a mount for an 81mm mortar. The mortar was added by divisional personnel but seems like a waste considering the limited firepower the mortar could bring to bear in comparison to size of the vehicle. (US Army)

Part of the crew of this M-41 watch as the howitzer is fired on enemy positions. The vehicle is from Battery B of the 999th Armored Field Artillery Battalion. The total crew of the M-41 numbered 12 men. Note how the howitzer has been camouflaged and a firing pit of sandbags has been built in case of enemy fire or possible ground attack by infiltrators. (US Army)

An M-46 from the First Marine Tank Battalion fires on Chinese positions. The use of sandbags helped protect some of the more damage-prone parts such as suspension, tracks, and bogey wheels from counter-battery fire. Shell containers have been used to hold the sand bags in place. (USMC)

Marines load 90mm ammunition into their M-46s after a fire-support mission in central Korea. The ammunition was in protective casings and shipped to the war zone in wooden crates which gave it a great deal of protection from rough handling. Note how the turret numbers are repeated on the front hull, and the addition of the Marine Corps insignia above the pioneer rack. (USMC)

The crew of this M32A1B3 do minor maintenance on their tank retriever in a camouflaged revetment near the front. In the primitive Korean countryside these tank retrievers proved to be invaluable. (USMC)

A Marine Amtrac on patrol north of Seoul sits in a village while the crew watches an air strike by Marine Corsairs on communist positions. The crew has attempted to break up the outline of the vehicle with mud dabbed on the sides and front, but the overall effect does not look too convincing. (USMC)

(Above) In the muddy terrain casualty evacuation was a serious problem. To help in this job this M-29 Weasel has been converted to the casualty evacuation role with the addition of four litters. (US Army)

An M-24 from the 45th Reconnaissance Company of the 45th Infantry Division fires on Chinese bunkers with the aid of an Army liaison plane overhead. The 45th Division was a National Guard unit from Oklahoma. (US Army)

Because of overwhelming UN superiority in armor, artillery and air-power the enemy usually attacked under the cover of darkness. To improve their nightfighting ability some tanks were fitted with searchlights to help. Though the lights were susceptible to enemy fire they proved their worth during the latter stages of the war. Initial trials started in the spring of 1952 when a shipment of General Electric search lights were received. (US Army)

(Right) In an attempt to counter enemy mines a number of different rollers were tested. However, much of the Korean terrain was unsuited for the rollers which easily became bogged down in the ever-present Korean mud. (USMC)

An M-39 moves back to the main line of resistance after a supply mission to a forward outpost. The M-39 proved very adept at carrying supplies up the steep Korean slopes when other vehicles were unable to do so. This particular carrier, nicknamed "Bouncing Betsy", was assigned to the 45th Reconnaissance Company, 45th Infantry Division. (US Army)

The crew of this LVT replenish their ammo supply during a lull in the fighting north of Seoul during the summer of 1952. Note the use of camouflage netting for overhead cover, additional sandbags atop the vehicle, and bunker for the crew to live in. Ammunition crates have been filled with dirt to provide extra protection between the vehicle and the bunker. (USMC)

(Left) A number of innovations were tested during the war. In an attempt to minimize engineer casualties when laying barbed wire under fire this M-4 was modified as a wire layer. The stakes to hold the wire were driven into the ground from the escape hatches in the tank's belly and as the tank backed away the wire caught on them. This was the theory. It did not work. (US Army)

As the Korean Army was reequipped some armor was provided to them. This M-36 Tank Destroyer from the Korean 53rd Tank Company sits in position prior to an attack by ROK infantry. With its 90mm gun the M-36 proved a good weapon for direct fire support when troops attacked enemy bunker positions. (US Army)

The crews of these ROK M-36s replenish their ammunition supply prior to a firing mission against Chinese positions on White Horse Mountain, north of Chorwon. The vehicles, from the 53rd Tank Battalion, carry a camouflage pattern of Earth Brown over Olive Drab. (US Army)

(Right) To protect the thinly armored sides of this M-4 from the 245th Tank Battalion, 45th Infantry Division (National Guard) has had angle irons welded to the fenders to hold logs in place. Note also how the crew has added a .30 caliber machine gun for use by the loader. (US Army)

"CUDDLES", a dozer Sherman from Lord Strathcona's Horse, digs out a defensive position along the Imjin sector of the front in the fall of 1951. In addition to the normal Canadian insignias, notice the small US star on the dozer blade attachment near the hull. (Public Archive Canada via Storey)

A number of different attempts were made to utilize the M-20 armored car in various roles. One such test involved the addition of a flame thrower in the fighting compartment. However the car's poor cross-country mobility, light armor, and open top made such usage a practical impossibility. (US Army)

(Right) Some of the jobs armor did were rather unusual. This Marine Amtrac has been pressed into service as an icebreaker to destroy ice floes which threaten the supports of the Spoonbill Bridge. This vehicle is an LVT-3C. 3C modifications included an enclosed machinegun turret and hatches over the rear troop compartment. (USMC)

Marine M-46s move up to the front line on a firing mission against newly discovered enemy positions. Rather than let tanks sit in front-line positions exposed to enemy fire, the sector commander often held them in reserve and only brought them forward when they were needed. Notice how most of the crew members are wearing their helmets for protection. (USMC)

The crew of "CYD CHARISSE" hold their ears as the their M-40 fires a 155 mm round at Chinese troops during a night assault. The self-propelled gun is from the 937th Field Artillery Battalion. Maximum range of a high explosive shell was over 25,000 yards. (US Army)

(Left) In an effort to combat guerrillas along rear supply routes some trains had armored railroad cars as part of their makeup. Though guerrillas were never a serious threat they did pose a problem, and guards were needed on all supply trains or convoys which moved in some areas of Korea. (US Army)

The crew of this M-16 fires on enemy positions near White Horse Ridge. The vehicle is from the 21st Anti-Aircraft Automatic Weapons Battalion (AAA WB), which was attached to the 25th Infantry Division, whose symbol, a Hawaiian taro leaf with a lightning bolt through it, is painted on the side. The leaf is Red while the outline and bolt are Yellow. Above the leaf is the vehicle's name, 'HELL'S FIRE'. (US Army)

During a lull in the fighting the crew of this M-40 clean the 155mm gun. When the front line became relatively static such prepared firing positions as this were a common sight. From such positions the entire front line was plotted so that when a firing mission was needed the time between the request and shells hitting the target was cut to a minimum. The bunker on the left holds ammunition and charges while ready rounds are in position at the right. (US Army)

(Right) In an effort to provide additional protection from enemy hand-held anti-tank weapons this Marine M-46 dozer has had a wire frame welded to the turret. In theory the wire would cause the anti-tank projectiles to detonate upon contact with the wire instead of the tank surface. However, by this time of the war (spring of 1953) there was not enough time left to effectively test such a theory and the idea was soon forgotten. Years later, in Vietnam, tank crews would use a similar idea which proved very effective against rocket-propelled grenades. (USMC)

This M-16, from the 21st AAA WB, takes part in a night firing mission against White Horse Ridge. It too carries the Taro Leaf of the 25th Infantry on its side. The stacks of .50 caliber ammunition boxes indicates the tremendous amount of ammo these halftracks could throw out in a relatively short period of time. The gun barrels would often glow White. (US Army)

Members of Lord Strathcona Horse, B Squadron, carry out a training exercise in late February, 1953. Note the diversity of equipment carried and the extensive use of track as extra armor. The Canadian M-8 in the foreground still carries US stars on its sides. (Public Archives Canada via Storey)

(Left) This M-4 has been modified to lay telephone wires to forward positions. The device in the front digs a small trench and lays wire in it; a small flange on the rear of the device pulls dirt back over the trench covering the wire. (US Army)

The last years of the war saw the front line take on the characteristics of trench warfare from World War One. These bunkers, belonging to the 2nd Infantry Division, sit just behind the main line of resistance. In some instances such bunkers even had paneled interiors! (US Army)

An M-20 armored car from the 563rd MP Company sits near ambulance buses which will take communist wounded to an exchange point at Panmunjom. For such duties as this or as convoy escorts the M-20 was adequate but in the field there was little the vehicle could do because of terrain conditions and the vehicle's inherent shortcomings. (US Army)

(Left) As the war began to wind down, every effort was made to keep up the troops' morale. This truck has been modified as a donut kitchen so that men in forward positions could have fresh donuts. The vehicle is from the 3rd Infantry Division whose insignia, a Blue square with White stripes, can be seen on the vehicle side. (US Army)

This tank retriever crew replaces a dozer blade on a Sherman. However, the blade will have to be turned around before it can be properly seated in the attachment on the suspension. The jury rigged wire rack on the side of the M-4's hull is a common modification made in the field. (USMC)

In an effort to provide additional illumination at night, searchlights were positioned on high ground. This searchlight truck from the 86th Searchlight Company sits atop a hill in the 3rd Infantry Division's sector. Even with camouflage netting such units were hard to conceal and were constantly moved to avoid enemy fire. (US Army)

As the war became static budget analysts found new ways to reduce costs. In an effort to save used brass shell casings tanks had brackets welded on their turrets to hold the old casings for return to the rear. As a side benefit a full container served as a crude form of spaced armor which could detonate incoming projectiles. The brace on the gun mantlet is for a searchlight. (USMC)

The crew of this M-41 from the 92nd Artillery Battalion fires the 300,000th round of artillery ammunition against communist forces. The gun was in the full recoil position at the moment the photo was taken. (US Army)

The UN had to guard against actions by South Korean civilians who were opposed to aspects of the peace accord. This M-20 armored car and M-16 halftrack guard the causeway to Wolmi-do Island where the UN Neutral Nations Supervisory Commission was billeted. This was done as a precaution against demonstrators in Inchon who were opposed to the commission and wanted its withdrawal. The M-20 is from the 8224th MP Security Detachment, while the M-16 is from the 50th Anti-Aircraft Battalion. (US Army)

(Left and Below) Even after the truce was signed an uneasy peace prevailed along the front. Both sides kept their forces in readiness in case fighting was renewed. (Left) An M-24 from the 40th Reconnaissance Company, 40th Infantry Division, sits under a camouflage net just south of the DMZ. (Below) The crew of an M-16 takes part in maneuvers with ROK troops. The vehicle is from the 50th AAA WB. (US Army)